# A Christian Spirituality
# and Psychotherapy

# A Christian Spirituality and Psychotherapy

*A Gay Psychologist's Practice of Clinical Theology*

RICHARD H. YORK

RESOURCE *Publications* · Eugene, Oregon

A CHRISTIAN SPIRITUALITY AND PSYCHOTHERAPY
A Gay Psychologist's Practice of Clinical Theology

Resource Publications
A division of Wipf and Stock Publishers
199 W. 8th Ave., Suite 3
Eugene, OR 97401

www.wipfandstock.com

ISBN 13: 978-1-55635-643-8

Manufactured in the U.S.A.

# Dedication

To Calvin E. Turley, DMin,
*My mentor who taught me what pastoral psychology can be.*

And

To Merle R. Jordan, ThD,
*My consultant who has journeyed with me through my doctorate
and some dark times writing this book.*

And

*To those lesbian women and gay men who strive to live
according to God's Covenant of love.*

# CONTENTS

# ACKNOWLEDGMENTS

I WANT TO GIVE special thanks to my copy editors, James Saslow, PhD, Julius Sokenu, PhD, and Steven Kagan, and to Merle R. Jordan, ThD who gave me much support by reading the whole manuscript and providing invaluable comments to make the text more clear and readable. However, if there are any remaining English language errors, they are Dr. Saslow's fault, but all brilliant insights are mine. After all, he called me an "impenetrable genius" when he could not understand something I wrote. After I picked myself up from the restaurant floor from laughing so hard, I said: *I agree*! Then told him he had to treat me accordingly.

I also wish to thank all those who read and gave feedback on various parts of this book and a conference presentation: Julius Sokenu, PhD, Peter McPherson, Joseph Cove, Russell Refino, Joseph Antao, Ronald Levasseur, Brent Slife, PhD, Fr. John Hogan, OFM, Fr. Frank Sevola, OFM, Fr. Stephen Lynch, OFM, Fr. Charles O'Connor, OFM, and the Mantalk group in New Bedford, Massachusetts, a gay men's support group. They gave me so much personal support for years that bolstered my self-esteem and helped me avoid falling victim to my old self-critical beliefs. They helped me heal and grow tremendously. These men are a part of the village that made me who I am today.

# INTRODUCTION

*The crucible of life's hurts and blessings orchestrated by God creates the alchemic heat to heal our wounds and transforms us into loving and caring people.*

I HAVE OFTEN ASKED myself, "Am I a fool for *Christ's* sake" or "a *fool*, for Christ's sake?" Here I am, seventy-one years old and writing a book about spirituality and psychotherapy, without ever being a college professor or publishing articles. I am no Mensa genius. My doctoral program in pastoral psychology did not assist me to integrate theological and spiritual concepts with psychology and psychotherapy. The theology I learned at Episcopal Divinity School was academic and not geared to helping people change their sinful behavior. I find writing very difficult. Sometimes I believe I am following God's call to describe a Christian spirituality and psychotherapy; other times, I simply want to give up and enjoy retirement. Sometimes when the writing got difficult, I asked myself, "Who do you think you are? You're not smart enough for this." And there it goes again. My old self-critic rears its ugly head.

I have persisted, however, because of the support from gay and straight friends, colleagues, and my Indwelling Spirit, my inner wisdom, which encouraged me to continue. They all helped me to realize that my perspective on Christian spirituality and psychotherapy was the *raison d'etre* of my life's journey. Fortunately, I learned I cannot do anything alone. For this reason, I often remind my clients that they cannot heal alone either. It became clear to me that we all need help from others and God in order to heal, grow, and do almost anything. Senator Hillary Clinton said it takes a village to raise a child; it took a village to produce this perspective. Dr. Calvin Turley, my mentor, often said we all stand on the shoulders of the ones who preceded us. I would not be here but for those who helped me heal and learn how to be a psychotherapist.

This book is a psychotheological reflection on my personal experience and the psychology and theology I learned on my journey. My conscious intention on this journey was to integrate my Christian theology and spirituality with my sexuality and what I learned in psychotherapy. This journey coincides with changing attitudes toward spirituality in the field of psychology: over the last few decades, many psychotherapists have developed spiritual perspectives in psychotherapy. I was able to become an effective psychotherapist because I was healed of the wounds created by past abuse and of other internalized images that led to self-destructive beliefs and behavior. I believe this healing came ultimately from my experience of Jesus Christ in the Holy Spirit of God as healer. This book is my witness to God's presence in my healing process and in the development of my psychotherapeutic perspective. I believe I am called to be a *clinical theologian*. That means I help people to learn how they block their spiritual and psychological healing by letting the past be the present, because they ignore the guidance of their Indwelling Spirit. I define clinical theology using theological, biblical, and spiritual concepts to describe psychological theory and psychotherapy.

Intellectually, this journey led me to develop a phenomenological perspective, not one based an empirical science, because I recognized that human beings are the products of their *experience in relationship*. It became clear to me that the experience anyone has in relationships involves spirituality and values. In the past, psychology totally rejected spirituality and values in favor of the presuppositions of empirical science, but I learned from my studies that we cannot be totally objective, as empirical science implies. I discovered that much of the knowledge I learned came from my experience in relationships, not empirical research; hence, my perspective is phenomenological, because human experience is the object of study in phenomenology. I believe empirical data is essential for psychology, but I do not believe that psychology can be inherently an empirical science (and I will explain why). I decided to redefine the philosophical foundation of psychology because defining spirituality as a relational concept was inconsistent with the epistemological foundation of contemporary psychology.

For philosophical reasons, I decided to include some of my personal experience on this journey and to identify how each experience influenced my perspective. This experience includes my relationships with God, friends, family, my therapists, and my clients, as well as what I learned in my professional training, various events of my life, and the answers to the questions I asked. I consider this experience to be essential data for my perspective because:

- It exposes my presuppositions.
- It shows how I arrived at certain notions.
- This journey of healing led to this perspective.

I believe it is more honest to describe the connection between my perspective and my personal and professional experience because most psychologists conceive their theories similarly; Sigmund Freud and Carl Jung certainly did.

My journey began because I could no longer tolerate the pain of my depression and anxiety. These overwhelming feelings of depression and anxiety were my response to internalized images created by the uncaring, abusive, conditionally loving relationships of my childhood experience. They were my defense against anger, shame, and guilt. These feelings and images were partly due to my relationship with my parents. My father was anti-Semitic, racist, insecure about his intelligence and masculinity, and often angry. He did not spend much time with me, and I never wanted to be a man like him. My mother wanted me to be her surrogate husband; I was the victim of covert incest. Even though my parents were loving in many ways, they used us children to satisfy many of their own needs, a pattern I learned about from the books by Alice Miller. They were both perfectionists, and I learned my lesson very well. They argued almost daily and would not allow us to express our anger; I repressed mine for years.

My early sexual experiences also produced other images and similar feelings. At nine years old, I was raped. As a young teenager, I started acting out with other teenagers and men. I became a sex addict, seeking friendship and love in self-destructive ways, but I can never remember feeling guilty about it until some kids in high school called me "queer." All through high school, and even into my doctoral program, I was tormented by the obsessive thought, "I am dumb," even though I was relatively successful in school and had earned two master's degrees by that time. I realized just recently, however, that *I* was the one who created that obsessive thought, because I had a reading comprehension problem; no one ever said that to me. (I have discovered many of my clients made similar conclusions about various self-esteem issues.)

Therefore, from my early childhood there was a conflict between my spirituality, my emotions, my self-esteem, and my sexuality. These conflicts were the result of my response to my parents, my sexual abusers, and my reading difficulty. The internalized images of these relationships became false gods, who tormented me all the time; I was guilty of idolatry as described by Merle Jordan (1986).

I also had other, life-giving relationships. My uncle and aunt who lived next door and the Episcopal Church were excellent examples of Christ-like giving and unconditional love; I usually attended the Eucharist with them at 8AM and sang in the church choir at 11AM. Their caring and loving relationship with me led me to become a churchgoer almost every week of my life. I learned from them that Christians could be caring and loving because of their commitment to the Church, as I experienced from others later. As a teenager one Easter Sunday, when I was alone in the church, I looked around and suddenly experienced a sense that coming here was important to my life. In the early 1960s, I came out for the first time when I moved in with my first lover. I can remember saying to myself that he was the first one to love me unconditionally, unlike my parents. Around that time, an Episcopal Benedictine monk gave a talk at my church that encouraged people to develop a prayer life and to become associates of the order. Since they were far away, I went with a gay couple to the Society of St. John the Evangelist (SSJE), an Episcopal religious order in Cambridge, Massachusetts, to investigate the possibility. I continued to visit the SSJE Monastery regularly by myself and began to meditate and pray daily; the fact that I was in a gay relationship was never an impediment to my relationship with the monks. Two years later, I joined SSJE and lived there for a year, but after I left, I disassociated myself from the gay men at Church and went back into the closet. However, I continued to meditate daily and read Evening Prayer using the daily lectionary, which I have continued to do almost every day for the last forty-five years. My experience in the monastery helped me feel better about my intelligence and removed some of the guilt for being gay.

Unlike most same-sex-oriented people, my experience with the Church was positive. After all, I was accepted to Episcopal Divinity School (EDS) as an openly gay man in 1970 and graduated in 1975. I got the courage to apply to EDS because I became a leader of the Homophile Union of Boston, a gay liberation organization that met at the church I attended in 1969. It was a sermon preached by Fr. Wessinger at St. John's Bowdoin Street, saying it was OK to be gay and Christian, which allowed me to come out a second time. The application to EDS required an autobiography, which I decided I could not write without describing my experience as a gay man and a Christian both past and present. I also said that my goal at EDS was to integrate my spirituality, sexuality, and experience in psychotherapy for personal and professional reasons. At that time, I wanted to become an Episcopal priest. Many of my papers at EDS were my first attempts at this integration, which culminated in my senior thesis (York, 1975).

The most persistent question on my journey since the early 1970s began in response to sermons admonishing us to be more loving. I would listen to sermons at St. John's Bowdoin Street and ask myself: "I believe it is possible to be as loving as you say, but how can I become more loving if your sermon doesn't help me?" I recognized I was self-centered and not very loving. It took me until the late 1990s to answer this question. I finally realized God dwells in us to help us to be more loving, and that God shares the pain we experience in relationships.

The great benefit of my depression, anxiety, and traumatic experiences was that my pain forced me to seek help and find healing. The most powerful influence in this healing process was the presence of God that I call the Indwelling Spirit. The initial awareness of this experience came from the Anglican theology and spiritual writings I read in the early 1960s. This theology emphasized that God was an indwelling presence. In the late 1970s, Cal Turley introduced me to the Higher Self concept in Roberto Assagioli's theory of psychosynthesis (1965).[1] Anglican theology and Assagioli's psychological theory led me to believe that all people have an inner wisdom, their Indwelling Spirit. I came to believe that Assagioli's Higher Self was the Christ within, even though I hated myself. I experienced my Indwelling Spirit as a guide and teacher that was totally different from my oppressive inner critic. I sometimes experienced an inner voice telling me what I did or said was either wrong or self-destructive, but I never felt put down as I did with my inner critic. Wisdom came to me from within, from my study, and from others, which helped me become healthier, more loving, less self-centered, and more moral. I recognized that this wisdom was similar to the wisdom referred to in the wisdom literature of the Old Testament. This wisdom leads, not only to knowledge of the created order, but also to relationships based on justice.

---

1. See chapter 2 for further explanation of Assagioli's concept of the Higher Self.

Encouraging this kind of wisdom is what dedicated psychotherapists also do, whether they realize it or not.

In the midst of my doctoral studies in 1982, I decided to become a Roman Catholic. I made this decision in part because the 1979 General Convention of the Episcopal Church passed Resolution A–53, section 3 that says, "We believe it is not appropriate for this Church to ordain a practicing homosexual."[2] I had already been rejected for ordination in three dioceses and another openly gay graduate from EDS was being abused in the process of being ordained. I had gone "over the hill" from St. John's Bowdoin Street to worship at the Paulist Center because that Roman Catholic congregation was more true to the social justice spirit of the Gospel. I went there in exile from the Episcopal Church for its ambivalence about social justice and homosexuality. I knew Christians who were anti-psychology and gay men who were anti-Christian. I felt torn between the Church, my vocation, my spirituality, my sexuality, and my problems with depression. I decided for the Roman Catholic Church because it was consistent about its beliefs and practice, unlike the Episcopal Church. Then it dawned on me one day: God was not calling me to be ordained; the One[3] was calling me to a ministry of psychotherapy. What a glorious relief! Although at times, there is that nagging question: Am I guilty of the Stockholm syndrome—identification with the oppressor?

In the late 1990s, I was preoccupied with answering two theological questions, whose answers had a profound influence on my healing and my concept of the Indwelling Spirit. I often asked God, What is the Good News? New moral principles from the Sermon on the Mount did not seem like Good News to me. What is the Good News in trying to figure out what is right and wrong all the time? That is perfectionism. For many years, I believed that Christianity was not *primarily* a religion of morality, but that did not answer my question. One day in meditation, it came to me: Christianity is primarily a religion of a new relationship with God, a God who showed us how much he loved us by being willing to die on the cross to relieve us of being enslaved to sin. As the Bible says, Christ loved

---

2. The General Convention 1979: House of Bishops. (1979) Resolution A–53. *Journal of the General Convention of the Episcopal Church in the United States of America.* New York: Seabury Professional Services, no 3, p. B–97.

3. I use "One" as the pronoun for God throughout this book to avoid referring to God with gender.

us when we were yet sinners. Morality proceeds out of our relationship with God, not the reverse. Rather, because we love God, we become more loving of God and others as a way to please the One. Otherwise, we would be striving to earn God's love. We are not people-pleasers; we are God-pleasers. In addition, God helps us to do that by helping us stop our sinful behavior. Certainly, we have a responsibility to use our will to make moral choices, but only God can give us the grace to transform us from sinners to saints. However, our wills are not free. We are compromised by sin and our trauma histories. God can reveal these blocks to us through his grace working in us and through others. This theology of the Good News is a theory of change in theological terms. Therefore, I contend that theology ought to be relational, not philosophical.

My second question to God was, how is the suffering many people experience be atonement for sin, particularly those who spent years of misery in the concentration camps during World War II? I could not believe that theologians would say these people were suffering because of their sins. They experienced excruciating pain and torture for years, much too long to atone for any sin: after all, Jesus was on the cross only three hours. Some of these people were in a misery similar to Jesus's suffering. Then it dawned on me: Christ's suffering on the cross was only one example of the constant suffering God experiences daily because Christ is present with us in our suffering and our sin. The Bible clearly says that we are the Temple of the Holy Spirit. God bears every pain with us, from the smallest cut to the most heinous assault. No one is ever alone in one's pain: God shares that pain with each of us, as well as our joys. In short, the Good News is that, in Christ Jesus, we have a new relationship with God, a God who shares our pains and joys, even though God knows we sin. It is a relationship of love and compassion with forgiveness for sins. We are asked to forgive others as God has forgiven us. Morality proceeds from our love of God, rather than God demanding we become moral before we receive the One's love. We cannot earn God's love because we already have it.

However, my experience in Christian communities and spiritual direction was not the primary source of my healing; my twelve-step program experience was. These programs have a very simple and integrated approach to spirituality and healing. At first, I thought that twelve-step programs were a substitute for psychotherapy. Later it became clear that psychotherapy and twelve-step programs help people in different ways.

Twelve-step programs are a way of life that can help people throughout their lives, while psychotherapy helps people to overcome their resistance to changing self-destructive behavior. Both psychotherapy and twelve-step programs help people get rid of automatic behavior patterns that inhibit them from having a truly free will. I learned that psychotherapy is often an essential adjunct to twelve-step programs, and have attempted to create Christian twelve-step groups.

In short, I am a village. Senator Hillary Clinton said it takes a village to raise a child. Many people contributed to who I am through a healing journey, which relieved me of chronic depression, anxiety, self-hatred, shame, slavery to compulsive sexual relationships, and perfectionism. This journey included almost daily meditation and prayer, hundreds of hours in psychotherapy, weekly attendance at the Eucharist, spiritual direction, many relationships with unconditionally loving people, twelve-step programs, and a relationship with my Indwelling Spirit. I became sick in relationships and I became healed through others. I am still striving to be well and develop as a psychotherapist. My experience has affected whom I treat and how I treat them. Hence, it is no surprise that I treat those who are victims of depression, anxiety, and sexual, emotional, and physical abuse, plus those who are sex and love addicts, substance abusers, and gay men and lesbian women who have psychological problems.

This book is a record of my reflections on my personal and professional experience that led to my Christian spirituality and psychotherapy perspective. I do not claim to provide an academic analysis of the development of spirituality in contemporary psychology or to offer a thorough literature search. I only refer to the many writers who have influenced my perspective. This document is essentially a psychotheological reflection on my experience. Some readers are probably wondering, why was it important for me to identify myself as a gay psychologist in the book's subtitle? The answer is in the chapter, "A Clinical Theology for Sexual Relationships."

# CRITIQUE OF PSYCHOLOGY

*My perspective is not a synthesis of knowledge: it is but one-way to the One who is the source of all knowledge and wisdom.*

## Brief History of the Relationship of Spirituality and Psychotherapy

HISTORICALLY, THERE WAS LITTLE relationship between spirituality, morality, and psychotherapy in mainstream psychology and pastoral counseling. There was little evidence that these disciplines acknowledged that values or spirituality had anything to do with psychotherapy. In fact, these disciplines considered any kind of spirituality, morality, or theology anathema until relatively recently.

This anathema was the result of the divorce of psychology from the discipline of philosophy in order to make psychology more scientific. However, it was not a total mistake because psychology became freed from the tyranny of traditional theological dogma and philosophies that no longer helped people cope with daily living. This divorce occurred around the turn of the twentieth century. James Mark Baldwin (1982), a pioneer in this transition, developed a cognitive-developmental psychology called genetic epistemology.[1] This freedom from philosophy allowed various schools of psychology to develop different theories and therapies that helped many people. Psychology became what philosophy once was, a discipline that united theory and praxis. Freud was one of the first to do this by establishing a theory of psychoanalysis with the goals of encouraging patients to love and work. Consequently, people were provided with

---

1. His theory is very similar to Piaget's, and is discussed in the next chapter, but he did not do research as Piaget did.

the opportunity to free themselves of inherent shame and guilt related to their humanity or sexuality without becoming irresponsible, unloving, or uncaring. They did not have to believe they were evil or sinful just because they were sexual beings and in pain. Various schools of psychology since Freud have sought to relieve human suffering from shame, guilt, unworthiness, unloveability, selfishness, aggression, addictions, perfectionism, co-dependency, and self-criticism, while various psychotherapies have healed many people of unnecessary suffering or allowed them to cope with their lives better.

Even though Freud and others rejected spiritual or moral concepts in their theories and therapies, their goals of therapy definitely were, at least as I define those concepts. Freud's goals for psychoanalysis were love and work. Bruno Bettelheim (1982) wrote an article in the *New Yorker* claiming that Freud's theory was misunderstood as anti-spiritual because the English text of Freud's theory translated the German words, *Ich* and *Es*, as *Ego* and *Id*, instead of *I* and *It*, which ignored the more spiritual meaning in the German. Other psychotherapy theories also had similar goals and concepts that can be described as spiritual and moral.

When I did the bibliographic research for presentations on spirituality and psychotherapy, I was working with sex offenders, raised issues of morality for me, but I assumed I would find few writings on spirituality, morality, and psychotherapy. To my surprise, in spite of the anti-spiritual attitude of psychology, many articles had been published about these issues from a variety of sources, even pastoral counseling, and some dating back to the 1960s. These publications described the essential elements of spirituality and greatly influenced the development of my perspective. Herbert Benson, MD and Bernie Siegel, MD have done much research and writing about healing medical conditions; Benson calls his approach "mindfulness," and his group still conducts workshops on this subject. He also has done research that identifies how meditation affects the body. There are many articles and books about values and morality in psychotherapy (Holmes & Lindley, 1989; Kelly & Strupp, 1992; Kitwood, 1990; Mullan, 1991; Nelson, 1994; Nicholas, 1987; Patterson, 1989; Prest & Kelly, 1993; Saucer, 1991; Whitehead & Whitehead, 1994; Wicks & Parsons, 1993; Wood, 1987; Worthington, 1993, to list a few).

Leo Rangell (1967, 1971, 1986) and those who wrote to honor him (Blum, Weinshel, & Rodman, 1989) are most significant, because he was a psychoanalyst. He described the essential nature of valuing and moral judgments in personality development and later life and decried the traditional, amoral stance of many psychoanalysts in this country.

Robert Francher (1995) described psychotherapy as effective primarily because the culture accepts the principles of psychotherapy: healing through psychotherapy works in this country because the culture at large accepts it as healing; i.e., believes that it works. Hence healing is possible because it is a community activity, a reality that provided further justification for my "community of healing" concept.

Other authors have addressed the spiritual aspect of psychotherapy directly. Roberto Assagioli (1965) developed a psychology that described a spiritual aspect of the self, which he called the *Higher Self*. The Higher Self guides and teaches the person on his or her journey. Groups of people established training centers to teach this perspective in Italy and this country, some of which still exist. Calvin Turley (1971) wrote his dissertation on the integration of psychosynthesis and Swedenborgian theology, which he called Theotherapy. He interpreted the Higher Self concept as an indwelling presence that helps people to regain their birthright and get out of the hells in which they live each day. He helped people recognize their personal theologies as a self-esteem system of thoughts and feelings, like "I'm dumb," "I'm incompetent, unworthy," and the behavior that acts them out. The degree of low or high self-esteem and the type of self-messages determine how self-destructive the person is. This theory has formed the foundation of my concept of the Indwelling Spirit.

Scott Peck (1978), a psychiatrist and psychotherapist, described an approach that integrated psychotherapy and Christian spiritual journey. He assumed no distinction between spirit and mind or between the processes of achieving spiritual growth and mental growth. He assumed they are the same and that this process is an arduous and lifelong task. For a time, he led very popular workshops, some of which focused on teaching people to build healing communities. He also wrote about evil (Peck, 1983) in a work I will refer to later.

Irving Rosen, MD spent most of his professional life treating people from a spiritual perspective and promoting the spiritual aspect of psychotherapy through seminars and presentations. Rosen (1991, 1993a, 1993b) considers spirituality difficult to define because he believes that it contains disparate elements. His model uses a spectrum of consciousness moving from the body to the ego level; he considers the Whole Person, Witnessing Self, and Beyond Self as the realm of the spiritual.

He describes treating anxiety states and the relation of psychiatry and religion as it relates to spirituality. He was trained as a psychoanalyst, but rejected psychoanalysis in the process of studying the religious worldview of the pastoral counselors who were his students at Boston State Hospital. He developed a spiritual perspective, whereas the pastoral counselors developed a psychoanalytic one.

In York (1987), I described a methodology to study bodyself-concept that defined both the spiritual and psychological aspects of bodyself-concept, and qualitative and quantitative data produced in a pilot research project. Even though my study used only a small sample, the factor analysis of the Q-sort did identify groups of people who had similar belief systems with obvious spiritual qualities. I defined the psychological aspect of bodyself-concept as the positive and negative attitudes people learn about their bodies that affect their self-image, and the spiritual aspect as the acceptance or rejection of their bodyself-image as it is over time.

Fritjof Capra, a physicist turned ecologist, was the first one to provide me with the concept of spirituality in terms of relationship. For Capra (1996, p. 7), the awareness of our connectedness with the cosmos is spiritual. This awareness makes our spirituality relational. He goes on to say that a paradigm shift is emerging that considers human beings to be a part of the web of life, not the center of it. He contends that since the scientific revolution in the seventeenth century, scientific facts were considered value free.

> Although much of the detailed research may not depend explicitly on the scientist's value system, the larger paradigm within which this research is pursued will never be value free. Scientists, therefore, are responsible for their research not only intellectually but also morally. Within the context of deep ecology, the view that values are inherent in all of living nature is grounded in the deep ecological, or spiritual, experience that nature and the self are one. (1996, pp. 11–12)

Capra also believes that ideas come from experience and are not derived from information, an insight that is an essential aspect of my own epistemology. (His insights are similar to Slife's hidden paradigm of psychology, discussed later in this chapter.)

Paul Moore (1992) says that symptoms like addictions, depression, and anxiety are the soul seeking to be heard. He claims that psychotherapists have been too willing to encourage symptom and pain relief, thereby depriving people of the opportunity for real growth in wisdom and change, i.e., permanent change. He believes psychological problems are challenges that require soul-searching, not just symptom relief. He considers healing to be a process where grace emerges as the person surrenders to the process. His work echoes Ecker and Hulley's (1996) symptom-based therapy. His "soul voice" is akin to my concept of the Indwelling Spirit working in psychotherapy.

Merle Jordan (1986) describes how we tend to idolize or idealize our parents and those who abused us when we were children. We internalize images of our parents and abusers, giving them ultimate authority over who we are and what we do. These images become our gods. He calls the attachment to these destructive internalized images the sin of idolatry, because these attachments violate the First Commandment: "Thou shalt not have other gods besides me" (Deut 5:7). The goal of psychotherapy is to free clients from their submission to these god-like, destructive, internalized images. His theory and psychotherapy method, based on Ecker and Hulley (1996), is the foundation of my perspective.

Bruce Ecker and Laurel Hulley (1996) describe their symptom-based therapy as different from solution-based therapy. Their approach assists clients to determine how they maintain their symptoms and what problem the symptom solves for them. Solution-based therapy attempts to find a way to stop the symptoms and gives suggestions on how to change the behavior—in other words, to solve the problem that clients face. Ecker and Hulley realized that clients resisted changing their behavior, and sought to find out why. Symptom-based therapy addresses the resistance to change, in other words, what keeps clients repeating their symptom. They use a form of questioning they call "radical inquiry," which assists clients to experience the attachment to internalized images, which keeps them repeating behavior or feelings that they do not want. They help clients discover:

- What the symptom does for them.

- Why they value it so much.

- How the symptom is a successful solution for some problem instead of a failure.

- What would happen to them if they did not have the symptom?

Although Ecker and Hulley do not say there approach is spiritual, I will describe how the process of radical inquiry is spiritual because it involves the Indwelling Spirit. I will also describe various techniques to help clients answer the above questions based on Ecker and Jordan.[2]

All these publications and others were very helpful in the early development of my perspective, but I didn't consider them representative of the views of the psychological establishment, such as the American Psychological Association (APA), or of pastoral counseling. So in my early writings I criticized psychology for the resistance to including spirituality as an aspect of human personality and psychotherapy, because my personal experience and reading taught me that spirituality was an essential part of me and all people. However, over the last ten years many psychotherapists have addressed the relationship between spirituality, human personality, and psychotherapy. In 1996, 1998, and 2000, there were conferences on the spiritual aspect of psychotherapy sponsored by the Danielson Institute, a pastoral counseling center at Boston University, to honor Dr. Merle Jordan. Around 1996, the Danielson Institute modified their training program in pastoral counseling to include explicit spiritual and theological issues. They also sponsored monthly seminars for clinicians from 2000 to 2002, which I attended. In 2003, the newsletter of the Religion and Psychology, Division 36 of the APA, had a number of articles on spirituality (Williamson, 2003). In 2003, Division 36 sponsored the first Mid-Year Research Conference on Religion and Spirituality at Loyola College in Maryland. Since 2003 there have been five conferences that presented research studies in spirituality, psychotherapy, and the psychology of religion, and the APA has published a number of books on spirituality and psychology.

So in general, there is now an acceptance that spirituality is a part of psychotherapy and human personality. Psychotherapists from all schools use psychotherapy to heal people and relieve their pain and suffering and I believe in the same goals. However, for me, psychotherapy is essentially a spiritual process, because it involves values and produces healthier relations with self and others that are accurately described as moral. In contrast, many psychotherapists conceive the process as only psychological and ignore the moral issues.

---

2. See the section, "Clinical Theology Practice Techniques," in chapter 8.

My current critique of psychology is that psychologists adopted a philosophical foundation for psychology that is antithetical to the goals of psychotherapy and ignores the fundamental reality that we are all relational beings who constantly deal with moral values. Instead, they decided to use the subject/object epistemology of rationalism as the philosophical foundation for psychology. They wanted to divorce themselves from religious or moral concepts primarily because they wanted psychology to be an empirical science in order to make it more respected, as Slife (2006b) says, and because they knew that religions had hurt many people. They did not want to deal with God and morality except in the psychology of religion and forensic psychology. My critique of psychology thus involves:

- The philosophical foundation of psychology.
- The definition of spirituality.
- The resistance to address evil.

I take it as fundamental that psychology cannot be an empirical science based on the subject/object epistemology of rationalism. It is a relational science: people are formed in relationships, they only live in relationships, and the goals of psychotherapy intend to help people live better in relationships. A relational science recognizes:

- That the object of study is human experience and the relationships we live in are called our *experience in relationships.*
- That the research methods are based on the assumption that objectivity is impossible.

This means that a subject/object epistemology is antithetical to the fundamental reality, or ontology, of human experience and the goals of psychotherapy. Relationships are the essence of human experience and personality, not empirical knowledge, even though research knowledge is essential for a viable discipline. Hence, I decided that a relational philosophical foundation for psychology made more sense. As a corollary, since I believe spirituality is an aspect of the relational experience of psychotherapy and human personality, I could not define spirituality based on the epistemology of rationalism. Spirituality must be a relational concept as well. Consequently, if psychology is fundamentally relational, morality and evil cannot be avoided in psychological discourse. Questions arise such as, How do people treat each other? Are they mean, abusive, and neglectful, or kind, caring, and life-giving? I also contend that psychologists adopted a rationalist worldview that is value-free to avoid dealing with the issues of morality and evil, which they relegated to religion. Yet clients present with feelings of guilt, shame, and mean behavior. These feelings and behavior are not purely religious issues; they are also psychological and spiritual, because they occur in response to our *experience in relationships.*

## The Rationalist Foundation of Psychology

Brent D. Slife (2006a) identified the hidden rationalist paradigm of psychology by contrasting the theistic worldview with the naturalist and deist worldviews. The naturalist worldview assumes that creation is godless, that natural laws and principles govern the universe, that world can be objectively observed, and that researchers strive to be value-free. The deist believes that the universe was created by God, but God no longer acts in world events. God created the universe like a machine with laws and principles that continue to work without God's intervention. This absence makes the deistic worldview similar to naturalism. In contrast to both of these systems, the theist worldview assumes that God created the world and continues to be involved in world events in some way in order to accomplish the One's will. Hence this worldview has an intrinsic teleology. Theism is in conflict with the other two worldviews because they reject value, meaning, the active force of God in the world, and a teleological goal within the created order. Slife (2006b) describes the hidden paradigm of naturalism that psychologists adopted to make psychology a science that excludes religious people, values, and meaning. He describes how this hidden "set of paradigmatic prejudices violates psychology's own code of ethics—the code that prohibits psychologists from discrimination against religious people" (p.1). He makes it clear that the assumptions of the naturalist worldview of psychology are values, and says this paradigm is prejudiced because:

- It is unexamined by psychologists.

- It claims privilege over other perspectives.

- It suppresses other points of view, particularly theism and the experience of our religious and spiritual clients.

Psychologists avoid identifying moral values in psychology but have always described behavior in value-laden terms. They describe behavior as healthy or unhealthy, self-destructive or self-loving, hurtful or caring. These descriptions look like value judgments to me. They are also moral judgments because they describe right and wrong if you use my definition of sin, i.e., hurting self or others. Also, it is clear that most people feel guilty about what they believe is wrong. Guilt is a common human experience and is an appropriate response to behavior that is destructive to self or others. For this reason, I do not believe psychologists want to stop everyone from feeling guilty about everything. Therefore, it seems dishonest for psychologists to ignore the obvious value and moral issues of human experience and base the discipline of psychology on the value-free assumptions of the naturalist worldview.

The naturalist worldview ignores the inherent value-centered core of human experience. It is obvious to me that almost all people, like myself, have moral values, make value judgments, and have a conscience. We feel guilty about doing wrong, and live by some Higher Power that encourages us to love and find a purpose in the world. These moral values and purpose imply the assumption that a Creator is behind them.

In fact, values are at the very core of why clients have problems. If clients did not have values or a conscience, they would have no conflicts at all. Most of their problems would not exist and they would do whatever they desired. Clients come to therapy because they have mixed feelings about what is right, good, or healthy for them. Therapists know that perfectionism and guilt feelings are pervasive in clients. Clients often ask: "Do I have to stay depressed, anxious, use drugs, or is there a better life for me?" Most of my clients, religious and nonreligious, spiritual and nonspiritual, want to be kind to themselves and others and want to be rid of painful feelings, but decide it is impossible to do so without help. They ask similar questions like, why was I abused? Why didn't God stop it? What is my reason for living? These questions are all about values, meaning, and purpose. Therefore, it seems common sense to say that values, meaning, purpose of life, and some form of Higher Power are fundamental aspects of human experience that need to be a part of psychological inquiry and treatment. If psychology avoids this reality by employing assumptions of value-free research methods and treatment, it is gaining knowledge that ignores the problems of our clients. How can psychology help clients address these questions if it rejects values, meaning, and purpose as core issues of study?

This discussion accentuates the differences between my theistic psychology and traditional psychology. Currently, psychology is founded on the godless, subject/object, and materialistic epistemology of naturalism. This paradigm ignores the reality that values and morals are intrinsic aspects of everyone's life, whereas a theistic psychology is founded on the assumption that God is present in creation and that sin and evil are real. Psychology tends to either ignore or have difficulty dealing with the reality of evil because it is founded on an ostensibly value-free, objective worldview in order to be allied with the methods of Newtonian physical sciences (Slife, 2006b, p. 2). My intent is to replace the naturalist foundation of psychology with the ontological principle of relationality because I believe that relationality better describes the reality of human life, as described in the next chapter.

## Remaining Issues of the Resistance to Spirituality in Psychology

Historically, the psychoanalytic theory of Sigmund Freud was anti-religious; until the last ten years, psychoanalysis considered its technique amoral. All psychologies considered any moral system or spirituality an imposition on the client. Even pastoral counseling disowned any theological or spiritual aspect of psychotherapy until the mid 1990s. Almost all schools of psychotherapy were similar until recently and did not consider spirituality as an aspect of human personality. This reluctance to define the spiritual aspect of psychotherapy has reduced the ability of psychotherapy to accomplish its goals, for four reasons.

First, denying that spiritual values are an inherent part of human personality is a denial of truth: almost all psychological problems have clear moral and/or spiritual elements. For example, self-hatred or self-criticism fixates people on negativity about themselves and others. At the very least, they ignore or minimize positive elements of self and the world around them, and sometimes they commit suicide. One of the characteristics of depression is despondency, another word for lack of hope. Hope is obviously a spiritual concept. Depression can also lead people to suicide, suicidal ideation, or the desire not to be alive. Most professionals consider sex offenders to be narcissistic, i.e., so self-centered that they have no empathy about how they hurt their victims. These examples are only a very few of the spiritual aspects of psychological problems that have moral implications. These are all moral issues, if sin and evil are defined as that which hurts self or others.

Secondly, and most important, I propose that healing in psychotherapy is provided by a Higher Power. Yet with true hubris, some therapists believe that the therapeutic relationship is the healing agent alone. I contend that healing is the result of the therapist, the client, and the Inner Wisdom of the client working in concert. Even many medical doctors acknowledge that healing is the result of some internal process that they only facilitate; they do not heal the patient. I call my Higher Power the Spirit of Christ in God, but most people use other concepts. I contend that denying clients direct knowledge of and contact with the healing powers of some form of Higher Power robs them and psychotherapists of the most powerful alliance for healing. Without a Higher Power, therapists and clients are left with a therapeutic process that is totally human and are often alone in their pain, feeling as though there is no love in the world except from other people. They do not learn that they are keeping themselves from this healing presence. This approach creates a form of solipsism in which clients are left "to pull themselves up by their own bootstraps," without ever knowing the magnificence of a healing power and the meaning it provides. When psychological healing is viewed as solely a human process, clients are robbed of the opportunity to know that there is a loving, caring presence within them that fosters their healing process, i.e., Moore's (1992) "soulfulness." It would be more effective to acknowledge and access this magnificent power rather than making healing solely dependent on the human relationship between the therapist and client. No one can become fully human by one's own efforts or any human effort alone. Our creation and our potential are gifts. It would seem that this wisdom ought to be a part of any theory of psychology or psychotherapy.

Thirdly, psychology without the moral aspect of spirituality creates intrapsychic and cultural compartmentalization. Most psychotherapists would agree that psychotherapy should encourage integration, not compartmentalization of one aspect of human experience. No compartmentalization would occur if religious and spiritual people only had moral questions. Yet people who are atheistic, agnostic, or anti-religious also make moral judgments and acknowledge they do bad things; most of my marginally religious or anti-religious clients have a well-developed moral sense. Therefore, morality is certainly a part of everyday experience, and to restrict it to religion only aids and abets compartmentalization. Consequently, psychology creates an intellectual ethos in the cultural consciousness that divorces morality from the individual psyche, thus placing it outside the purview of psychology. This ethos exacerbates societal problems by separating psychology from religion in the collective and personal psyche. If people go to therapists to deal with their emotional problems and to religion to deal with their moral ones, they dichotomize what is essentially a unitary experience. This segregation ignores the fact that people cannot be moral, in the religious sense, unless they deal with their dysfunctional behavior and are healed of various psychological wounds. Many conservative Christians fall victim to this compartmentalization and do not seek psychotherapy because they believe that psychology is amoral, valueless, and Godless, yet they desperately need a trained psychotherapist to help them deal with their problems, not an untrained pastoral minister. I believe that much of the violence we face in our schools—such as in Littleton, Colorado; Conyers, Georgia, and elsewhere—is a result of this compartmentalization.

Fourthly, the psychotherapeutic enterprise does not encourage the formation of a community to support progress during therapy or after people terminate. When people leave therapy sessions, they often return to the settings that created the problems or to their own private misery. They need a support system to facilitate their newfound growth. I believe that psychotherapy is only a jump-start to healing; permanent change is a lifelong process. Sometimes people are kept in therapy too long because the goal is to completely solve their problems; people need to continue the growth process after terminating therapy. Even the psychoanalytic goals of *love and work* take a lifetime. Moreover, therapy is necessarily very expensive; hence, the working poor often have difficulty getting the expert help they need.

To provide support for lifetime healing and growth, I believe that psychotherapists and pastoral ministers should encourage the formation of healing communities. These communities would function like twelve-step programs. They would develop a set of principles that guide and support lifetime healing and permanent change of behavior. The principles would acknowledge the spiritual, psychological, and physical aspects of personality. In addition to the traditional forms of therapy, workshops and retreats could be used. Members would participate as long as they needed the help; people could come and go as needed. The major focus would be to develop a community of healing that fosters a psychospiritual way of life according to identified principles, (not moral rules), and uses everyday life as the crucible of healing, all under the guidance of some form of Higher Power. These groups would be spiritually based for non-religious people but could also be religiously connected. They would help people deal with their sin and evil in order to become more loving and healthy. Prophetically, in my 1971 autobiography letter to EDS, I said my goal in seminary was to learn how to develop a ministry within a parish community that is much the same as these communities of healing.

## Brief History of Christian Spirituality Movements and Pastoral Counseling

There were a few early attempts to create healing communities. Protestant churches used Christian spirituality as a source of "mental healing" start-ing in the mid-to-late-nineteenth century. Hunsberger (2005) says that some Protestant ministers of that era formed an alliance with scientific psychology in an effort to understand how their religious beliefs could help their parishioners with their mental illnesses. Christian Science and the New Thought were movements that sprang up from the same ethos; while they used Christian spirituality and theology, they did not use medicine in their approach as the Protestant ministers did. In the early twentieth century, Protestant ministers who followed in the footsteps of this alliance were instrumental in the acceptance of the psychoanalysis of Sigmund Freud.

Another movement started within the same ethos. Kurtz (1979, p. 9) tells the story of the relationship of the Oxford Group and its influence on the founding of Alcoholics Anonymous (AA). While neither group was explicitly therapeutic, both provided much healing for non-alcoholics and alcoholics. The Oxford Group was a non-denominational and evan-gelical movement that attempted to recreate early Christianity. It began as The First Century Christian Fellowship in 1908. Its headquarters were in New York City at the Calvary Episcopal Church, where Rev. Dr. Samuel Shoemaker was rector.[3] The movement did not focus on alcoholics, but

---

3. Later he moved to Pittsburgh, Pennsylvania and started another community move-ment that was based on Christian principles, but not the Oxford Movement ones.

many members were recovering; Bill Wilson and Dr. Bob Smith, who later founded AA, both maintained their sobriety by going to these meetings.

The Oxford Group believed in divine guidance, although abuses caused group leaders to advise members to check this "guidance" with the group. They followed four absolutes: absolute unselfishness, absolute honesty, absolute purity, and absolute love. Because of these absolutes, Bill Wilson found them too moralistic, judgmental, and preachy; he also disliked their contention that their way was the *only* way to solve problems. He left the Oxford Movement to create AA, where he and other early AA members created a twelve-step program to avoid these pitfalls, which they felt were counterproductive to achieving sobriety. However, the four Oxford principles found their way into AA, minus the "absolute" demand, except for absolute honesty.

The Emmanuel Movement (1904–1929), a therapeutic movement that had similarities to AA, was also influential in the formation of AA. It began in the Emmanuel Episcopal Church on Newbury Street in Boston, Massachusetts when Rev. Elwood Worcester became rector in 1904. According to Hunsberger (2005), Worchester and Dr. Samuel McComb had studied the "new psychology" in Germany and current developments in abnormal psychology and neurology. They were trying to put the treatment of mental health using spiritual principles on a scientific foundation. Their approach was an integration of Christian spirituality, medicine, and psychiatry for the treatment of physical, emotional, and spiritual problems. They used counseling and hypnotic suggestion as a part of their therapy. Worcester started working with McComb, Dr. Richard Cabot, and other medical doctors to treat people with tuberculosis at the Wednesday Evening Health Service. Later a psychiatrist, Dr. Isador H. Coriat, joined them and taught courses on mental disorders. Their treatment was a combination of fellowship, a simple form of lay psychotherapy, and teaching about medicine and Christian spirituality— an early form of group therapy. They found that many of the people they worked with were alcoholics and discovered that these people could remain sober if they participated in the program. This movement was very much like AA without the twelve steps. The early members of AA, such as Bill Wilson and Roland H., attended these meetings. The Emmanuel Movement was an attempt to overcome the divisions between religion and medicine already evident at the time. Hunsberger (2005) says that this movement paved the way for the acceptance of psychoanalysis in

Protestant circles and laid the foundation for modern pastoral counseling in this country (p. 8). However, some professionals on all sides questioned the religious, psychiatric, and medical orthodoxy of the program. Unfortunately, the movement died out shortly after Rev. Worcester retired from Emmanuel Church in 1929, probably because there was criticism of its scientific rationale and the competence of the therapists, and because it was an attempt at an integration of spirituality and medicine when the dominant ethos of the time was empirical science. Later these same issues infected the pastoral counseling movement.

Dr. Frank Lake was one of the pioneers of pastoral counseling in the United Kingdom. He was an English physician who later trained as a psychiatrist. He integrated Christian theology and spirituality with psychiatry starting in the late 1950s and published *Clinical Theology* in 1966. His psychology was eclectic; initially he used object relations theory but later introduced Carl Rogers, Eric Berne, and Fritz Perls. He believed Jesus was the model for a healthy person and used the Christian Gospel as a means to bring healing to people. Lake called his developmental theory the Dynamic Cycle. It was based on his view that Jesus was secure in his identity because he was rooted in God: when Jesus became exhausted in his ministry, he would pray to regain his strength. Lake created seminars for training clergy and started the Clinical Theology Association, now the Bridge Pastoral Foundation,[4] in 1962 because he discovered that clergy received no training in seminary to deal with the problems their parishioners faced. He was accepted by many but criticized by others for creating a hermeneutical problem by saying modern psychological concepts existed in the biblical record. I avoided this hermeneutical problem by defining the Indwelling Spirit as a psychological phenomenon people experience today based on biblical and theological concepts from the Judeo-Christian Tradition.[5]

Another movement that started as integrative of Christian spirituality and psychiatry was Clinical Pastoral Education (CPE), established by Anton T. Boisen (1876–1965) as a training program for clergy and seminarians. He was an ordained Congregational/Presbyterian minister who became catatonic in the early 1920s and was hospitalized twice at

---

4. The Bridge Pastoral Foundation website: www.bridgepastoral.org.uk/franklake .html, was the source of this information.

5. I address this hermeneutical problem in chapter 6, "The Indwelling Spirit Concept."

Worcester State Hospital for many months. After his recovery, he was invited to be the hospital chaplain there in 1925. His intention was to overcome the divisions between religion and medicine by using the "living documents" of patients to learn about religious experience. He was a researcher of religious experience, not a clinician. His approach was decidedly Christian, as is evident in his statement of belief in *The Exploration of the Inner World* (1936, p. 296), which begins by acknowledging the love that rescued him on the first Easter morning. He felt forgiven for his sins and failings by the life and teaching of Jesus Christ. He said that from the beginning of Christianity, the strong gave to the weak and God was hidden in the disguise of the weak and imperfect. Now it is time for the weak and imperfect to give their lives for the strong so that the divine can be freed from "the prison house of deformity" and love can fully reign to overcome the violence and repression of our society.[6] His successor in 1931, the Rev. Carroll Wise, decided to make the program clinical as a way to train seminarians and pastoral ministers to do pastoral counseling. This change eventually led ministers in the CPE movement to abandon their Christian spiritual and theological roots in pastoral counseling. Towards the end of his life, Anton Boisen lamented this loss. CPE spawned many organizations throughout the United States that certified training programs for pastoral counselors. Some theological schools opened pastoral counseling centers, such as the Danielson Institute at Boston University and the psychology department at Andover Newton Seminary.

The pastoral counselors' disconnection from their Christian roots was described by Paul Pruyser in his presentation at the Lowell Lectures at Boston University in 1975.[7] Pruyser (1976) gave a not-so-subtle critique of pastoral counselors from his experience of teaching them as director of professional training at the Menninger Foundation in Kansas since

6. I have kept a copy of this Statement of Belief in my wallet for years. Every time I read it, I cry because I identify with the weak and imperfect people he mentions: I too have been labeled as sick and/or evil because I am gay.

7. This critique did not affect the teaching of the pastoral counseling department of Boston University at all at this time. I was studying for a master's degree at that time but did not attend this lecture, unfortunately. If I had, I would have known then that pastoral counseling was not integrative of theology and spirituality. I believed that since Cal Turley was a pastoral counselor who had integrated spirituality and psychotherapy, a pastoral counseling program would be a good place to learn more about this integration; unfortunately, however, it did not occur until the mid-1990s, as I describe below.

the late 1940s. (By this time, CPE had taken root in many seminaries in this country.) He and Karl Menninger acted as consultants for chaplains working in hospitals where they had psychiatric residents, seminarians, and pastors meet together for seminars and consultation about patients. He discovered that the theologians acted as though they were "sitting at the feet of the psychiatric Gamaliels,"[8] (p. 23) while the psychiatric professionals thought that the ministers had their own concepts, traditions, and practices but did not talk about them. In fact, however, when the theological professionals were encouraged to conceptualize patients' concerns in theological terms, they would either ignore the clear spiritual and faith issues or translate them into psychological language; they lacked the language to talk with people in theological terms. The theological professionals seemed to distrust people's faith issues and instead translated the issues into family therapy, conflicts with parents, or psychodynamic issues. They did not see the theological processes in the problems of their patients or parishioners. Pruyser was surprised that theological professionals no longer knew their basic science of theology. He said it was about time that pastoral counselors returned to their roots.

I experienced this disconnection from Christian roots in my own CPE programs. One program was at Worcester State Hospital, Massachusetts, which I attended as a seminarian in the summer of 1972. There was no instruction about Christian spirituality or theology in chaplaincy, but we were expected to function as chaplains with clinical knowledge. There were, however, classes on psychoanalytic theory that provided clinical knowledge. This teaching reflected the psychoanalytic foundation of pastoral counseling in the northeast.[9] We did learn about Anton Boisen and I read portions of his chart from his commitment there that referred to his Christian beliefs and Christ's ministry to the sick. An extreme sign of this disconnection occurred in another CPE program at Massachusetts General Hospital, where the director said we become God to the patients. This was repugnant to me because I believed it was blasphemy and the

8. Gamaliel was the wise Pharisee in Acts 5:34, who told the Sanhedrin not to interfere with the Apostles because if they did, the Sanhedrin would be fighting against the power of God, while if they did not, the movement would fade.

9. Pruyser (1976) said that the psychological theory and methodology used in the Midwest was from Carl Rogers, not from psychoanalysis as it was in northeastern pastoral counseling programs.

height of hubris. He never talked about Christian theology or chaplains as ministers of the Gospel in a hospital setting, or about how God worked through us, but he was willing to say we became God to patients. He substituted us for God's presence.

I believe pastoral counselors abandoned their prophetic role to be healers with Christ. They ceded their profession to a psychological establishment that was anti-religious and anti-spiritual. They succeeded at being very competent clinicians but suffered from the fear that psychologists would not accept them if they talked about spirituality or theology. Yet they were ordained ministers of many Protestant denominations and Roman Catholic and Episcopal priests and religious. In reality, they became psychologists who were pastoral ministers. The question of competence in pastoral counseling, which started with the Emmanuel Movement, lingered into the 1980s. For example, when I was a student in the pastoral counseling program at Boston University in the early 1980s, one of my professors wrote a paper on the immanence and transcendence of psychotherapy. He did not include even the word *God* in the paper, in spite of the fact that these concepts were clearly theological. When I asked him why he did not, he said that he was afraid of what his colleagues would think about him. A decade later, I discovered he had overcome this fear when he made a presentation that demonstrated that he valued the relationship between spirituality, theology, and pastoral counseling. He probably always did privately.

This failure to integrate theological, spiritual, and psychological language into pastoral counseling persisted until the mid-1980s when there was an explosion of writings on spirituality and psychotherapy from pastoral counseling circles. Until that time, pastoral counselors acknowledged qualities of the psychotherapy relationship, such as compassion, self-love, being nonjudgmental, inclusion, openness, confidentiality, and respect, but would not call them Christian. In a conversation following the 2000 Spiritual Aspect of Psychotherapy Conference at Boston University, Carole Bohn, who was then the executive director of the Danielson Institute at Boston University, admitted that historically, pastoral counselors were more concerned about competence as clinicians than about their Christian theological or spiritual roots. However, by then the Danielson Institute had developed a program that integrated spiritual and theological issues into their training. This change came because the fellows of the Institute from the psychology department asked why the

Institute did not address spiritual and theological concerns. She was very instrumental in the process of developing the spiritual dimensions of the Institute's programs. Now, the web site of the Danielson Institute program describes the Practical Training program and the Predoctoral Psychology program as opportunities to explore "the interface of psychology and theology/spiritual perspectives."[10]

Despite my desire to integrate spirituality and psychotherapy, in the spring of 2006, I was appalled to discover that I was guilty of succumbing to the need to be a competent therapist just like other pastoral counselors. I found myself more worried about trying to do symptom-based therapy than about developing the use of the Indwelling Spirit in psychotherapy sessions, even though this is my primary contribution to the profession. At that time, I was down to five client hours a week and felt anxiety due to financial insecurity and incompetence, a recurring theme in my life. In my meditation it dawned on me that I was not focusing on using the Indwelling Spirit in my sessions. To help me focus, I developed the pages about the Indwelling Spirit that are in Appendix B. Within days I started to get referrals, and my practice mushroomed. I believe that this crisis happened because I was not doing what God intended me to do. My Indwelling Spirit allowed me to experience the anxiety to get me to ask God what the problem was and taught me that I was more focused on being a competent therapist than developing the Indwelling Spirit concept for psychotherapy. The vestiges of my sense of incompetence and financial insecurity drove me to focus on being a competent therapist instead of listening to my Indwelling Spirit.

## The Absence of Sin and Evil in Traditional Psychology

As I said above, most psychologists and pastoral counselors until recently avoided referring to sin and evil like the plague. There were some good reasons for this: historically, pastoral ministers were judgmental when they told someone that she or he had sinned. As a result, they encouraged people to hold onto guilt and shame and to believe they were bad persons because they sinned. There was no distinction between the sin and the sinner, particularly about sexual sins. Psychologists wanted

10. The Danielson Institute website address www.bu.edu/danielson/training/predoc .html.

to avoid being judgmental and to find the motivation for destructive behavior in order to promote healing and health, but these pastoral ministers were more concerned about people being moral than they were about healing past wounds.

There were some notable exceptions to this avoidance. Carl Jung and his Jungian followers have written many volumes and articles about spirituality, sin, religion, and the problem of evil in the shadow side of our personality. Jung considered his analytic approach a spiritual process, which is exemplified by Jung's treatment with Roland H., a severe alcoholic. After many years of analysis, he told Roland that he could not remain sober unless he had a spiritual or religious experience—a conversion. In AA, this conversion became known as a spiritual awakening. According to Kurtz (1979),[11] this analysis by Jung became one of the "founding moments" of AA through the correspondence between Bill Wilson, the founder of AA, and Jung. Because I knew this history, the Jungian perspective was very compatible with my thinking in the late 1970s, so I joined a Jungian study group and planned to study in Zurich. I even visited Aniela Jaffe, Jung's biographer, and the Jung Institute in Zurich, Switzerland.[12] But I gave up the idea when I discovered that the members of my study group were having difficulty understanding the Jungian study materials even though we all had graduate degrees. I then started searching for a simpler methodology for psychotherapy.

Karl Menninger, in *Whatever Became of Sin?* (1973), says that therapists no longer describe behavior as sinful or evil, and ignore the consequences of sin and evil. He says that instead of calling it sin, psychoanalysts call behavior that hurts another person "aggression" or, if it hurts oneself, "self-destructive." Calling this behavior a crime or a symptom is a substitute for calling it *sin*. Menninger says that the failure to identify sin and evil led people to disown responsibility for their behavior. Consequently, patients often look upon sin as fun instead of feeling guilty about doing something wrong. I have often heard people say, "I'm naughty," or gay men say, "I'm a slut," and feel proud of it, not guilty.

11. Kurtz refers to letters between Bill Wilson, the founder of AA, and Jung to establish that Jung's analysis of Roland H. was a key element in the founding of AA.

12. On my visit in the summer of 1974, I asked her whether Jung was a Christian or not. She said he was a Christian believer, but not a church-going.

There have been significant attempts to develop a psychology of evil. Paul Sanford (1981), for example, describes an ontology of evil for psychology using Christian and Jungian concepts. He describes evil as real but mysterious, a product of the shadow side of consciousness from a Jungian perspective. Scott Peck (1983) writes about the need for a psychology of evil and the dangers of articulating one. He warns us about the human tendency to point out evil in others in order to avoid the evil within ourselves, and about the danger to any researcher who attempts to investigate evil.

However, the problem is that the psychological mainstream has refused to embrace any notion of the psychology of evil or sin. As Karl Menninger says, sexual offenses and other antisocial behavior, like Jeffrey Dahmer's murders, are identified as mental illness or crime, not evil. Many defendants in court cases use the insanity plea to explain murder as "brief psychosis." Many analyses of the Columbine High School massacre described the behavior of the killers as mental illness. They ignored television reports that said that the killers were satanic worshippers. Few reporters referred to this report. The media blamed the families, video games, guns, or a culture of violence. Ironically, according to reports, all these factors were true. But the real point was missed. They explained this behavior in psychological terms, not as *evil,* most likely because the prevailing psychological ethos in society forbids it. Even if those killers were not satanic worshippers, there is no doubt they espoused white supremacy beliefs of hatred. These beliefs are not mental illness; they are decisions to hate independent of mental illness. These decisions are evil because the killers made repeated choices over a period of time, independent of any psychological etiology, to consider hatred as good. The criteria of hatred and lack of compassion for people are good criteria for judging behavior as evil. Kernberg (1993) calls these personality traits *malignant narcissism.* I believe it ought to be called evil behavior as well.

The Achilles heel of modern psychology is this refusal to describe a psychology of evil and to include some form of Higher Power in psychological theory and psychotherapy. These thinkers do not acknowledge that evil and sin are real or that they exist in the human psyche or in the cultural consciousness. Human behavior is considered deviant or destructive and is explained by theories of family origin, genetics, psychosis, other mental illness, or decision and intent. I believe this dissociation of sin and evil from psychology has led to a culture that allows evil to surface in new ways. Destructive behaviors against self and others are considered to come from the individual who commits them and not the transpersonal cultural consciousness. It is true that the etiology of sins in individuals can be explained. Yet to explain behavior in purely psychological terms leads to the banality of sin and evil. Without a concept of evil, evil becomes benign on the surface but gains power over people's lives like other repressed and suppressed content. Murder/suicides, domestic violence, children killing children, parents killing children, and pedophile murders have increased dramatically in recent years. The increase in these crimes cannot be explained only in terms of the offenders' family of origin or genetics. They are the result of evil emerging from the collective unconscious because modern psychology has reduced sin and evil to some form of psychodynamics and has divorced morality from spirituality in human psychological theory.

Psychologists forget that all people deal with shame and guilt. These feelings cannot be relegated to religion or theology; they are psychotheological issues. Even pseudoguilt is a psychotheological issue. Feelings of guilt and shame lead to sinful behavior[13] because they affect how individuals relate to others and every other aspect of their lives. Almost everyone who comes into psychotherapy suffers from guilt and shame. If these feelings are the result of abuse or neglect, people tend to act out with drugs, alcohol, gambling, stealing, compulsive shopping, or compulsive sexual behavior as a way to medicate the pain created by their experience. Some people get involved in destructive relationships in search for love. These behaviors are compensation for the abuse and the love they never got. These behaviors are sin and evil because they are destructive to self and others and sometimes crimes also. I believe in calling a spade a spade.

Yet some data already exists that could help create a psychology of sin and evil. Forensic psychology has much research data and experience in differentiating mental illness from criminality. One of the jobs of forensic psychologists is to assess whether people are responding to hallucinations or paranoia, or whether they deliberately choose to hurt someone for selfish, sadistic, or other motives. Their assessment determines if people are criminally mentally ill or criminally narcissistic. Criminal narcissism is committing acts with no empathy for the victim or

---

13. Below I define sin as behavior and attachments to images that are destructive to self or others.

satisfying only selfish desires. They also determine if someone is sexually or violently dangerous. Criminal mental illness is responding to auditory hallucinations or psychotic paranoia such as a mother killing her children because she heard voices telling her to do it. This experience has created much research data and literature that can be used to determine whether behavior is sinful or evil.

Creating a psychology of evil is not a goal of this book. My conclusion at this time, however, is that evil is a malevolent force that affects all people in different ways depending on their experience in relationships. Destructive self-esteem images are the major conduits that evil forces use to lead people to sin and self-destruction.[14] Three excellent criteria for defining evil behavior are:

1. A lack of empathy for the victim.

2. The belief that it is acceptable to hate groups such as Afro-Americans, Jews, same-sex-oriented people, and foreigners.

3. A premeditated decision by the perpetrator to satisfy his or her own sexual and aggressive needs only.

However, more research needs to be done in order to make an authoritative determination of these criteria. Peck's (1986) warning about the researchers involved with researching evil needs to be heeded. Research on evil behavior needs to be done by those who are willing to engage those who participate in it. These researchers need to be well-differentiated individuals to avoid being contaminated by evil, otherwise they will become like those vice squad police who take bribes from the drug dealers they pursue or protect them. It is imperative that psychology as a profession begin to address the problem of evil, for the health of our cultural and individual psyches. The research needs to answer the questions: What is evil behavior? Can a person become evil and if so when does that happen? Can a person be released from being possessed by evil or when is one lost to it? These answers will affect forensic psychology and much of psychotherapy.

To address my critique of the spiritual aspect of psychology and psychotherapy, my goals for the rest of this book is:

---

14. The destructive self-esteem images as conduits of evil are discussed in chapter 8.

1. To describe a relational philosophical foundation for psychology and spirituality.

2. To describe a theistic psychology that contains some form of a Higher Power.

3. To define theology in relational terms and a new task for theology.

4. To define the moral element in spirituality for psychology and psychotherapy.

5. To integrate psychological, theological, and spiritual terms into a constructionist theory and practice of psychotherapy.

These definitions would facilitate a new relationship between philosophy, psychology, and theology without creating one discipline as there was before the turn of the twentieth century. However, if psychologists wish to address the divorce of morality and evil from psychology and psychotherapy, a multidisciplinary approach would be best to develop these definitions. Following is my resolution of that divorce.

## 2

# A NEW PHILOSPHICAL BASIS FOR PSYCHOLOGY

THE LAST CHAPTER ANALYZED the empirical-science foundation of psychology and the consequences of not including morality as a part of spirituality in psychological theory. Modern psychology was placed on a scientific foundation towards the end of the nineteenth century when the early psychologists decided to separate psychology from philosophy. They wanted a scientific foundation for psychology like that of the medical and physical sciences in order to put psychology on par with these disciplines. They wanted to use empirical methods to gain knowledge, whereas philosophers used rational discourse only. As in the other sciences, psychologists chose the epistemological approach of logical positivism as the foundation of research. I claim that this epistemological approach is inappropriate as a foundation for psychology because all psychological knowledge deals solely with relationships, whether the subject is perception, cognition, or psychotherapy.

## Brief Historical Background

A pioneer in establishing the epistemological foundation of psychology was James Mark Baldwin. He was trained as a philosopher and wrote the book, *Social and Ethical Interpretations in Mental Development: A Study in Social Psychology* in 1897. This book was the beginning of his work on a genetic epistemology, an experimental philosophy. According to Broughton and Freeman-Moir (1982), Baldwin did not do empirical research because these methods were not available at the time; instead, he concentrated on building his theory of genetic epistemology. He tried to maintain the relationship between psychology and philosophy when G. S. Hall and others were trying to liberate psychology from metaphysics and epistemology, but Baldwin is little known because he did not pursue

33

empirical research (1982, p. 4). John B. Watson, Ivan Pavlov, and B. F. Skinner developed the behaviorist approach through their research in the early part of the twentieth century. Even though the behaviorist approach dealt primarily with conditioning, this process involves relationships, not subjects separated from objects. Their approach was not totally objective.

In the mid-twentieth century, Piaget's work had striking similarities to Baldwin's, although historical links cannot be proven. Piaget (1964/1967) also called himself a genetic epistemologist. His research "restore[d] the connection between science and theory of knowledge, a connection so willingly and deliberately dismantled by the last few generations" (Broughton & Freeman-Moir, 1982, pp. 1–2). Both of these men were concerned about moral, cognitive, and affective development. Ironically, some of the beginnings of psychology were concerned about elements that can now be considered spiritual.

## Critique of Psychology as an Empirical Science

I have already said that no epistemological approach can provide an appropriate philosophical foundation for psychology or psychotherapy, or for the spirituality aspect of psychotherapy. Thought and knowledge are certainly real, but they are not a fundamental reality of human personality or human experience. Relationships are. We live for some time after birth before we start thinking or gaining knowledge, in contrast to Descartes' claim, "I think therefore I am." We are the products of many relationships. Spirituality is about relationships; i.e., relationship with self, others, the created order, and some form of a Higher Power. Human beings are created from some form of relationship. It is also true philosophically that all knowledge is created in relationships and that what is observed in research is a relationship with something. To separate knowledge into a subject and an object creates a fundamental distortion, not a fundamental reality.

Rejecting a logical positivist approach to research, however, does not mean that empirical research is worthless. Research is essential for psychology[1] and psychotherapists. The current methods are essential to determine that data are valid through statistical analysis. Also, healing

---

1. Although this book is not about empirical research, I argue that it is possible to research spirituality if the theory of psychology is based on abstractions of human experience.

in psychotherapy is facilitated by the knowledge therapists gain from research, training, and study. However, it is not empirical knowledge that makes psychotherapy work. It is the therapeutic relationship that facilitates healing and growth, regardless of the school of psychotherapy. This relationship promotes healing because the therapist listens to, guides, and cares for the client and the client knows this. Because of the therapeutic relationship, clients learn how they resist healing and to find the answers within themselves.

Psychology is not a physical science nor is it an art. Psychotherapy and psychology are relational sciences. The goal of psychotherapy is to lead clients to have healthier life-giving relationships with themselves and others. Hence, psychotherapy is essentially a relational process that uses scientific knowledge to facilitate the therapeutic relationship. This process demands an explicit relational, philosophical base and relational research methods. Logical positivism, the philosophical base of empirical research, cannot provide such a foundation. In fact, logical positivism is alien to psychotherapeutic relationships because it is based on non-relational, epistemological assumptions; i.e., subject/object and thought/feeling dichotomies. Psychology needs to champion the eradication of dualism, not perpetuate it.

In the last chapter, I summarized Brent Slife's argument that psychology is based on a rationalism that accepts a subject/object method of gaining knowledge or, in other words, a subject/object epistemology. First, I believe it is impossible for any human being to be objective as empirical science claims. Many contemporary thinkers agree, such as Harry Oliver (1981), Fritjof Capra (1996), and Brent Slife (2005, 2006a, 2006b), to mention only a few. I have adopted a concept of subjective objectivity from Cal Turley to describe psychological research and psychotherapeutic relationships. I claim that knowledge is always gained through relationships with others, with self, and in training and through study, reading, and seeking answers to questions. Without acknowledging it, empirical researchers create knowledge through relationships even when they use rationalist subject/object epistemological assumptions. The perceptions of researchers are prejudiced by their experience and their unconscious or articulated worldview. No one can ever be truly objective because we cannot separate ourselves from our experience in any way, nor do I wish to. Relational research methods need to be developed that acknowledge these limitations of human perception. We psychotherapists have to learn about our vulnerabilities (our blind spots or assumptions) and how they can affect our psychotherapy. We strive to prevent ourselves from imposing our experience or worldview on clients or expecting them to satisfy our needs, except of course to pay our bills. These vulnerabilities are called countertransference. I strive to maintain an objective/observer approach, balancing empathy for clients with the knowledge of my countertransference vulnerabilities.

Secondly, I claim that the philosophical foundation of psychology ought to reflect the reality of what is studied. Psychology is fundamentally the study of human beings, who are products of relationships. In philosophy, ontology is about fundamentals, and epistemology is about what we know and how we know it. Hence, I contend that ontology should be the philosophical foundation for psychology, not the subject/object epistemology of rationalism. This epistemology distorts reality by creating a dichotomy that is not real. Oliver says, "Epistemological questions begin by bifurcating reality into knower-known" (1981, p. 1). This bifurcation eliminates any connection between the knower and the known and usually makes the knower (the therapist) more powerful or privileged than the known (the client).

Thirdly, the subject/object epistemology of rationalism and logical positivism was built on the epistemology of Descartes. His famous answer to the epistemological question, "What can I know?" was, "I think, therefore I am." His philosophy helped create a cultural ethos that values thinking over feeling. His epistemology is the apogee of the whole western philosophical tradition that preceded him. This tradition was founded on Greek philosophy that assumed a mind/matter dualism in which matter was evil and mind was good. Aristotle even said feelings could not be trusted. Later philosophers from Aquinas to Kant (and numerous others) built on this foundation by rejecting the notion that matter was evil. Yet they created a subject/object worldview in their philosophies. This philosophical base objectifies reality, which leads people to objectify themselves and others. This worldview also created a thought/feeling dichotomy that many people suffer from today, and is one of the primary problems we face in psychotherapy. It has produced a culture that values thought over feeling, encourages the compartmentalization of feelings dissociated from thought, and assists people to repress unacceptable parts of their experience. The self and others become objects, not relationships.

Psychotherapy is designed to help people overcome this objectification and repression. So why use a philosophy that supports objectification and repression? In reality, this philosophical view is alien to what therapists do. We strive to help people live in healthy, loving, and caring relationships. Hence, I claim that empirical science based on epistemology cannot be the sole foundation for psychotherapy or other aspects of psychology. Scientific research is an essential tool for psychology, but the epistemological assumptions of empirical science cannot be the foundation for the discipline because they obfuscate the reality (the truth) that relationships constitute the essence of human personality and experience. To avoid the subject/object problem, the discipline has the obligation to seek a relational basis for psychology, in order to be true to the goals of psychotherapy and to human experience, and to create new research methods. I conclude that the ontological fundamental for psychology is a relational ontology.

I first discovered this relational ontology while studying with Harry Oliver in 1978, who describes a relational ontology in his *Relational Metaphysics* (1981). To avoid the subject/object problem, he starts with the more fundamental metaphysical question: "What are the fundamentals of reality and being?" "Metaphysics is in fact the quest for fundamentals, i.e., for those entities that are irreducible" (Oliver, 1981, p. 176). He based his metaphysics on the new paradigm emerging from research in physics, which emphasizes relationality over discrete objective entities. Oliver's (1981) relational metaphysics considers relationship as the fundamental. He explains experience as follows:

> It has been customary to assume that "experience," i.e., experiencing, is what an "experiencer" does. There must first be the experiencer, then the experiencing. Such a commonplace misconception has produced the extreme of the absolute ego or consciousness. One might ask: How can there be experiencing without an experiencer? In my view, it is equally cogent to reply with the question: How can there be an experiencer without experiencing? Both questions combine to point beyond their limitations to a larger insight, namely, that experiencer-experiencing-experienced expresses a unity. (pp. 177–78)

Oliver means that human beings are essentially indivisible relations by essence. He defines the relational self with a notion of mutuality derived from Martin Buber's "I-Thou." For him, "the self does not *have*, but *is* its experiences ... the self *is* what it is doing" (Oliver, 1981, p. 179). Some have asked, what is a relationship? A relationship is *the one* experiencing *the other*. My study with Oliver convinced me that his ontology had powerful implications for psychology.[2]

From a similar perspective, Capra (1996) identified the problem of the self and the Cartesian subject/object problem. He says that Descartes' philosophy encouraged western thought to believe people and things are separate objects. The self was also an object. If objects are conceived as separate things, they belong to an objective world that exists independent of each individual. He said we need to shift our thinking from objects to relationships in order to overcome the belief that we are separate and independent of each other (p. 295). Capra (1996) also believes that ideas are derived from experience and not from information. This claim from Capra and Oliver encouraged me to make *experience* a fundamental concept of my perspective. Hence, my concepts and theories point towards people's *experience in relationships*. However, in concert with the mindset of these philosophies, it is essential to remember that these concepts are only signs, which point to the experience they describe. It is a grave mistake to reify abstractions.

Brent Slife explores the fundamental of relationships in his article, *Relational Ontology* (2005). He claims a relational ontology for psychology through an analysis of traditional notions of psychotherapy practice. He identifies abstractionism as the traditional ontology of the practice of psychotherapy. "With abstractionism, psychologists have generally assumed that abstractions, such as theories, techniques, and principles, capture and embody the fundamentally real" (p. 1). However, these abstractions are created by stripping away the specifics of people's experience through research studies. Abstractions thus become divorced from being fundamentally real because they lose their relationship to real experience; i.e., their context. Psychologists learn these abstractions in their training; in psychotherapy, they tailor these abstractions to help clients with their problems. This conception of practice means that psychotherapy becomes an application of abstractions to a concrete situation. Slife identifies many writers who have questioned this conception of practice. He concludes

---

2. I tried to encourage him to make this connection to psychology explicit, but he became involved in family issues and eventually moved to Georgia before we could work on this connection.

that "practices are inextricably intertwined with their concrete contexts and cultures, they cannot be abstracted from them" (p. 2). In other words, psychotherapy practice cannot be conceived as applying abstractions that are divorced from their context. Theories and techniques abstracted from their context cannot be real because these abstractions are a part of a larger whole, and each behavior is related to the other parts of the context. Psychotherapy is a relational process that by definition treats relationships: he describes each person as a "nexus of relationships" (p. 4). He describes how abstractionism creates the subject/object problem and the atomistic self for traditional psychology, in contrast to the relationships that are a fundamental reality for all people. He contrasts the relationalist and abstractionist views of community: the relationalist perceives that we are the product of a community that is constituted on the principles of love, intimacy, and closeness, whereas the abstractionist conceives a community as adhering to common beliefs and the avoidance of conflict in order to maintain the community. He concludes that relationality is the ontology for psychology, not abstractionism. This critique is an extension of Slife's critique of rationalism as the philosophical base for psychology (described in the last chapter), in which he exposes the values and beliefs within the presuppositions of rationalism.

Slife's critique of the practice of psychotherapy abstractionism reminded me of how I conceive the practice of psychotherapy. In our training as psychologists, we learn theories, techniques, and principles that become biologically programmed into our minds as knowledge. This program of knowledge allows us to organize what we hear clients say in order to make assessments and treatment. This program is a listening device, not a means to tailor or adapt theories to a client's problem as abstractionists do. The internalized knowledge functions like an enzyme. The substrates (what clients say) become organized along the enzyme (the therapist's programmed mind) that connects them and produces a new biochemical (a theory about what the client means). The difference between the abstractionist and my relationalist perspective is that abstractionism focuses on adapting the theories to the client and relationalism focuses on the connection to the client, which is, in fact, what most psychotherapists do.

Hence, the concepts of *relationality* and *experience* are the building blocks for a new philosophical foundation for psychology and the spiritual aspect of psychotherapy. One possible ontological fundamental is,

"I was conceived therefore I am." This ontological assumption is a better representation of human experience than the epistemological assumption, "I think, therefore I am," because:

1. It is the irreducible aspect of all persons who were born.[3]

2. It is inherently relational.

3. It is a sign of some relationship between nature and nurture.

Epistemological assumptions based on thinking cannot be irreducible fundamentals for psychology because they are based on mental operations that do not occur until relatively late in human development. Conception is considered a good ontological fundamental because it fulfills the philosophical requirement to be irreducible. No person would be born without being first conceived from some form of sex act (artificial or coital). Each of us is the result of a union between an egg and a sperm *plus* our responses to all of our relationships both mental and physical since that conception. The most important relationships are those with our parents, families, abusers, and other significant people. Those responses are programmed biochemically into the body. These programmed responses and the behavior that acts them out comprise the *relational self*. This means that the structure of each person—the body/self—is *embodied relationship*, not discrete unrelated entities, following Oliver and Capra. I conclude that "I was conceived therefore I am." is a better philosophical foundation for psychology than, "I think therefore I am." because it describes "what is real" and it is irreducible in both psychological and biological terms. It combines both nature and nurture. Each of us is conceived as a result of some sort of relationship between a man and a woman and the families, present and past, who raised them. I wrote the following poem to make clear my thoughts:

> We all live today, our body/self acting,
>     composite of all relationships since conception;
> reactions to all that has happened to us,
>     back through the wombs, loins, and
> lives of our fathers, mothers, grandfathers, grandmothers, ad infinitum
>     to the beginning act of creation.
> Each of us is relationship, relationship with all and all that is.

---

3. This ontological statement could be used to say abortion is immoral. I avoid this conclusion by identifying the statement with people after birth.

## The Relational Self

The *relational self* concept is defined on the foundation of relational ontology. The relational self is the primary concept of my spirituality and psychotherapy perspective, and is defined with psychological and spiritual concepts. The relational self concept is intended to describe the psychological and spiritual aspects of our personalities. These aspects are not discrete or separate parts of our personalities or our current experience. Each relationship that becomes internalized has both psychological and spiritual aspects. Psychologists and others can only describe the spiritual and psychological aspects of our personalities as conceptual abstractions, but these concepts do not represent reality; they are only abstractions that *point to* the psychological and spiritual aspects of our personalities and experience. The diagram below illustrates the relational self with all its components.

# THE RELATIONAL SELF

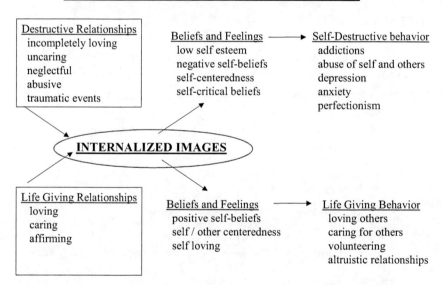

FIGURE 1. This diagram shows that the life-giving and destructive relationships become internalized images and our responses to these images create the beliefs and feelings. Together they form a neuropsychological program, which programs the corresponding behavior.[4]

---

4. This figure was created by my Power Point Wizard, Ronald Levasseur.

The psychological concept of the relational self is the structure of our personalities created by the internalization of our experience in relationships. This structure consists of the internalized images of all our experience in relationship since conception, plus the genetic inheritance that affects our behavior such as mental illness. Our experience includes all relationships with parents, grandparents, aunts, uncles, next-door neighbors, and those who abused us, starting from our birth. As one client said, these relationships are internalized as composite snapshots of what happened to us in those relationships. These relationships, not just the object of the relationship, become internalized or imprinted as images on various parts of our nervous system, creating a neuropsychological program.[5] Our nervous system is like a sponge that absorbs the feelings and thoughts about our relationships.

The spiritual concept of the relational self is the composite image or self-image created by our response to the internalized images. It is the spirit or essence of the person. It is what we become in response to the internalizing of the images. The spiritual aspect of our self-image is an expression of what kind of person we are and how we treat ourselves, others, creatures, society, the world, and some power greater than oneself, even if the person is an atheist. The caring and loving relationships assist us to love others and ourselves. The abusive and neglectful relationships lead us to abuse others and ourselves in various ways. The spiritual aspect of the relational self includes:

- Our learned moral system and our value system that is not moral.

- The degree of our self-centeredness and loving care for others.

- The meaning we give life.

- Our self-beliefs, feelings, and the behavior that act out the internalized images.

- The power greater than ourselves that we were taught.

The Indwelling Spirit is not included as a part of the spiritual aspect of the relational self because it was not produced by internalized images. The Indwelling Spirit is an inherent part of us since conception and is not

---

5. Chapter 8 describes why both poles of a relationship are internalized.

a product of our experience.[6] However, there appears to be some connection between the Indwelling Spirit and the internalized images. We know this to be true because people know what is right or healthy but may do the opposite instead. For example, "I shouldn't do drugs, but I did." The "I shouldn't" is the knowledge that drug use is not good. The "but I did" is acting out some internalized image. A perfect example of this kind of experience was with a depressed alcoholic client when he was about to enter a bar. His depression was due to feelings of self-hatred. He said, "It was like someone was next to me telling me 'don't go in' but I ignored the voice. I didn't want to hear it. I physically turned away from it because I could not stand those bad feelings any longer." His Indwelling Spirit was trying to guide him away from doing what he knew was wrong, but his need to get away from his feelings caused him to ignore that wisdom. His attachment to the internalized images was stronger than his Indwelling Spirit.

The Indwelling Spirit also consists of our ability to know right from wrong—our conscience. We were created with the ability to be caring, loving, and just, but the destructive parts of neuropsychological program block our access to always being good.[7] We are identified with or attached to our internalized images instead of our Indwelling Spirit. We can learn to remove these blocks that I call attachments in order to become altruistically caring and loving of self and others.

Our neuropsychological programs produce mental operations that are idiosyncratic to each one of us, such as feelings, thoughts, attitudes, core belief systems, value systems, value judgments, and worldview. These mental operations are acted out in our behavior, functioning as a complex of systems in our day-to-day experience. These systems are neither logical nor well integrated; some parts of the program are dissociated from the others. I use the word *program* because it conveys the sense that our behavior is determined by what we believe. Hence, the internalized images of this program determine much of our behavior.

---

6. The inherent nature of the Indwelling Spirit is an assumption of my psychology. Since it is an assumption, its presence cannot be questioned in empirical research. However, it can be an object of research because it is a phenomenon in everyone's experience in some form. This issue is described more fully in the chapter 6.

7. I discuss this inhibition of the Indwelling Spirit as my definition of *original sin* in the chapter on the theology of my perspective.

These neuropsychological programs produce our life-giving and self-destructive beliefs, feelings, and behaviors. Our experiences in loving, caring relationships and events coalesce to form a neuropsychological program that produces healthy beliefs and moral behavior—the life-giving responses. These responses are automatic in various situations but do not create problems for us because these beliefs and behavior become loving and caring behavior. In contrast, the traumatic and unloving experiences coalesce to form a separate neuropsychological program that produces self-destructive beliefs and behavior. As we grow older, these programs take on a life of their own, totally independent of the relationships that created them. This knowledge is important in psychotherapy, because many clients believe they are being forced to confront their parents of abusers, whereas they are actually dealing with the internalized images, not the persons who created them.

However, people do not have to have critical or abusive relationships to develop self-destructive beliefs, feelings, and behaviors. Some of my clients did not have abusive or severely traumatic family relationships, but exhibit self-destructive beliefs and behavior. They were victims of mental illness, of being assigned a caretaker role because of a parent's death, or of neglect due to demands of a sick or a mentally retarded sibling. These early relationships created internalized images similar to the ones created by destructive relationships.

Our neuropsychological program is set in motion automatically by present situations. These present responses are *"emotionally reminiscent situations."*[8] Our feelings become separated from the behavioral responses and most often are unconscious. Our self-destructive behavior responses are most often more powerful than our life-giving behavior responses. Most of us know what I am describing: have not some of us vowed as kids, "I'll never be like *them*!" (our parents). As adults, in horror, we hear ourselves saying those exact things we hated: "I can't believe it. I'm acting just like my mother." On the other hand, some of us rebel against teachers or bosses as we did with our parents. We are conditioned by our relationships like Pavlov's dogs or Skinner's pigeons. The self-image aspect of our neuropsychological program also has purpose and meaning: in other words, it has a teleological intent. The teleological intent of this self-critical belief system is to prove we are unlovable—a self-fulfilling

---

8. I learned this term from Cal Turley, my mentor.

prophecy. If we believe we are unlovable, we act out a system of thoughts, feelings, and behavior that expresses this belief. We say and do things with others that prove we are unlovable. This self-critical belief system at best hurts us. It often creates depression that can lead to suicide.

To be even more sinister and demonic, a self-critical belief system takes on a life of its own after we create it; we become self-critical of things we never heard from anyone. This system cycles every success or failure through its critical filter. For instance, I was never called *dumb* by anyone; in fact, I was considered smart by my peers in high school and was on the honor roll. Yet I was tormented for much of my life with the obsessive thought, "I am dumb," until about 10 years ago. After my second master's degree, a supervisor chided me by saying, "Maybe if you get a few more masters degrees and a few doctorates, *then* you will feel smart." Empirical evidence did not change my core belief. I was convinced, just as my clients are. Recently, I discovered that *I* was the one who concluded I was dumb because I had a problem with reading comprehension, as did a couple of family members. When I told this story to clients, they said they had similar experiences with reading or other issues.

We do not choose uncaring or abusive parents or others who abuse us, so we do not have to blame ourselves for their abuse or for even enjoying some part of that experience. However, we cannot blame others for our behavior. When these relationships become imprinted in our neuropsychological program as the relational self, *we* collude with them, *we* give them power, and *we* act out with destructive behavior: no one else can be blamed. These images are more powerful in our lives than the positive internalized images. They give us little or no choice in our behavior while we are attached to them. We act out our attachment to the idolatrous images in self-destructive addictions, rages, or other abusive behavior. We probably find ourselves acting like the abusive or uncaring people, but we cannot blame them for our abusive behavior towards self or others. We need to own our behavior. Owning our behavior is a major goal of my psychotherapeutic method.

As Figure 1 illustrates, the relational self contains images from both caring, loving relationships and from incompletely[9] loving, uncaring, unloving, abusive, or neglectful ones. Parents or other caretakers and

9. I use the terms "incompletely loving" or "completely loving" rather than "perfectly loving" to avoid any implication of perfectionism, which is discussed in chapter 4.

early abusive relationships are given ultimate power and have the greatest effect on the construction of the relational self. Because children idolize or idealize parents and abusers, the internalized uncaring, unloving, or abusive images become self-destructive. Our long ago response to these self-destructive internalized images produced our self-beliefs and behavior: we gave our power over to them, and they became the center of our lives. As we grew older, we continued to keep them in power over us and our relationships. We gave them ultimate authority as if they were idols, like those in the Old Testament. Recently a client defined an idol as "giving value to something that has no value"—an incredibly perceptive description of psychological idol worship. This "worship" or attachment to our internalized image idols makes us guilty of idolatry, following Jordan (1986), because it violates the first commandment: "You shall not have other gods besides me" (Deut 5:7). Therefore, this attachment is considered sin[10] because our attachment to these idolatrous images is acted out as compulsive self-destructive behavior. We act out of these attachments as if we were robots following a program. In effect, we worship these idols. These self-beliefs function like the rules of a fascist religion. The internalized images have so much power over us because they represent a basic need that insists on being satisfied. However, we are not doomed to live by these belief systems forever: psychotherapy can help release us from their captivity.

I conceive of belief systems as a composite of self-beliefs and behavior because the beliefs seem to program corresponding behavior, automatically. If I believe the self-belief that "I am dumb," I feel depressed, incompetent, and usually get very anxious in public settings. I do not do the work that would show that I am smart. The self-belief is a thought/feeling that leads to the behavior, and the behavior becomes a self-fulfilling prophecy of the belief. Self-beliefs produce misery if they are self-critical, self-hating, or self-destructive, and produce happiness if they are life-giving.

The connection of our experience in childhood relationships to our behavior later in life is clearly described by a print I have in my office:

---

10. I will elaborate on the connection of sin and idolatrous, internalized images in chapter 5.

## CHILDREN LEARN WHAT THEY LIVE[11]

If a child lives with criticism, he learns to condemn.
If a child lives with hostility, he learns to fight.
If a child lives with ridicule, he learns to be shy.
If a child lives with shame, he learns to feel guilty.
If a child lives with tolerance, he learns to be patient.
If a child lives with encouragement, he learns confidence.
If a child lives with praise, he learns to appreciate.
If a child lives with fairness, he learns justice.
If a child lives with security, he learns to have faith.
If a child lives with approval, he learns to like himself.
If a child lives with acceptance and friendship, he learns to find
    love in the world.

These sentences eloquently express how abusive relationships produce self-destructive behavior and caring relationships produce life-giving behavior.

Although our self-belief systems pertain to us, they also affect how we treat others. If we are critical of ourselves, we are usually critical of others as well. If we feel powerless, we sometimes compensate by judging others. Treating others as we treat ourselves is really an expression of the summary of the law: Love your neighbor as yourself. The way we treat ourselves is the way we treat others. If we do not love ourselves, in truth, we do not love others. The summary of the law is a true equation. Most therapists are quite aware of this dynamic and try to make clients aware of it. Moral theologians and pastoral ministers need to use this knowledge in their work as well.

I call our destructive self-belief systems our *personal heresy*. They consist of our self-destructive beliefs crafted out of our experience in relationships. Jordan (1986) uses the term *operational theology* with the same definition to differentiate the theology we learned in religious education from the theology we created in response to our experience in relationships. Originally, I used the term *personal theology* as a dedication to my mentor, Cal Turley, who used it effectively with others and me. I now prefer the term *personal heresy* because our self-destructive beliefs are antithetical to Christian theology, or heretical theology. Cal Turley made me aware of my own personal heresy in 1976 when he said, "You know, Dick,

---

11. I first saw this print on the wall of Cal Turley's office. The author is anonymous.

you believe in a loving God but you hate yourself." I was flabbergasted that I had not recognized this before. After all, by then I had had hundreds of hours of therapy, many confessions where I felt forgiven, hours of spiritual direction, had earned two theological master's degrees, and had written papers about the need to internalize theology. I even knew that self-hatred was the opposite of the healthy self-love. From reading Anglican theology and Irenaeus of Lyon, I knew that God loved, forgive, and was present within me to transform me into a loving person. God was never punishing nor a bearded old man ensconced only on a throne in the heavens. God was never dead for me, as many theologians of the 1960s believed. However, my personal heresy contradicted what I had learned. I believed that I had to earn God's love. It was not a gift of Christ on the Cross, because I had sinned by being gay and acting out sexually. Self-hatred was my only choice. At that time, I blamed all my life problems on being gay: if I were not gay, I would not be depressed, incompetent, and stupid, and would be a priest. My attachment to idolatrous images from my parents, my rapist, and my rejecting peers programmed these beliefs and behavior.

Personal heresy involves both conscious and unconscious beliefs, which both the privileged and the less fortunate develop. Some people who experience caring and loving relationships develop healthy self-belief systems, not personal heresy, because they believe, "I was given so much that I need to give to others." However, some from similar privileged families believe they are better than people who become alcoholics, drug addicts, prostitutes, homeless, or mentally ill in response to their *abusive* relationships. The privileged believe, "I am better than those reprobates," whereas those who are victims of abusive relationships believe, "I am not worthy of God's (or anyone's) love because I was abused." All these beliefs are profoundly spiritual and theological. Some victims believe that they are bad because they let the abuse happen, and thus are unworthy of the unconditional love of God. They cannot love themselves and often turn to drugs or alcohol. Either they believe they caused the abuse in some way or they blame God for letting it happen. I have heard many clients say, "Why didn't God stop _____ from happening?" These beliefs cause people to completely reject God and religion, or support self-hatred, or both. Family members and other men abused one of my clients, Maria. She refused to forgive herself because she did not tell anyone. She asked why God did not stop the abuse. In addition, her mother accused her of seducing her abuser. Her personal heresy was a belief that she was bad and unforgivable. Her attachment to these abusive relationships maintained that belief.

These two examples mean that psychotherapists and researchers can help clients identify their personal heresy so that they can learn the difference between their self-destructive personal heresy and life-giving Christian theology. Identifying this difference in theologies could help heal clients and produce research studies. The personal heresy concept is consistent with Kelly's (1965) notion of *personal constructs,* which has a valid research history; his method could be used in a research study on spirituality and behavior. My concept of self-belief systems would be an advantage in this research because self-beliefs program behaviors, thereby connecting personal construct theory with corresponding behavior.

This discussion makes it clear why psychologists find it so difficult to define spirituality: because the neuropsychological program has no separate spiritual and psychological experience. There is only one neuropsychological program with both spiritual and psychological aspects, which are only differentiated through abstract concepts, and are not experienced as different parts of the self. The psychological aspect of the relational self refers to "what we experienced in relationships;" i.e., the structure of the self that contains all the internalized images from our relationships. The spiritual aspect of the relational self refers to the self-image that we created in response to our experience in relationship: how we treat ourselves, others, the earth, social systems, and our Higher Power; i.e., what we became as a response to our internalized images. Hence, the relational self is comprised of a system of internalized images that can be described with both psychological and spiritual concepts. The relational self is the center of current and past experience.

Similarly, psychologists have difficulty saying that the spiritual aspect of our personalities includes morality because there are various forms of value judgments. If you say, "I like rock music but I hate Bach," these value judgments are personal preferences (unless you assault someone who likes Bach), not moral judgments. However, "I hate myself" is a moral judgment, because it becomes a core belief that leads to self-destructive behavior and sometimes suicide. This belief was *personally constructed*[12] from experience in relationships. Hence, this value judgment has a

12. This is a reference to George Kelly's personal construct theory.

psychological origin that leads to behavior that involves morality. This value is best described as psychospiritual.

Psychotherapy releases us from the captivity of our idolatrous internalized images and allows us to listen to our Indwelling Spirit. Since we constructed our personalities in response to our relationships, we also can learn to detach from our self-destructive constructs to live a healthy, moral, and loving way of life. Psychotherapy provides relationships with therapists who listen empathically. These new relationships help us to learn how to live in the here and now, free from destructive automatic behaviors, conflicts, and internalized images learned in the past. The psychological aspect of psychotherapy involves deconstructing the idolatrous internalized images; the spiritual aspect of psychotherapy involves learning how to listen to our Indwelling Spirit. To facilitate this process, the therapist aligns with the healing power in clients from the beginning and guides them towards the wisdom contained in their problems. The Indwelling Spirit emerges during the struggle with the problem. It provides healing, guidance, wisdom, and a sense of safety amid the destructiveness of internalized belief systems and world events. Problems and pain are opportunities for growth and healing or for danger and continued suffering. We can learn that the world is made for us as well as others—that we can be safe, productive, and not lonely, even if we do not have a spouse or a partner. Psychotherapy can assist us to grow from self-centered gratification of needs to a balance of love of self and others plus some kind of relationship with our Indwelling Spirit. Hence, I define spirituality in relational terms:

> Our spirituality includes those attachments to life-giving and idolatrous images from our experience in relationships as well as our relationship with our Indwelling Spirit who guides, teaches, heals, affirms and forgives us. Our spirituality has both positive and negative qualities because we are just and do good as well as sin. As we give up any sense of privilege and our idolatrous attachments, we become more loving, caring, and compassionate towards self, others, the created order, and society; and we become thankful for our relationship with some form of Higher Power.

## Other Philosophical Issues

Since this description raises the question, so what? Most therapists do the same thing with the exception of the Indwelling Spirit. What difference does it make that I use my definition of the spiritual aspect of human personality in psychotherapy? The answer is that the process of healing and growth in psychotherapy is inhibited when the presence of the Indwelling Spirit is ignored. It is hubris for psychotherapists to assume that a human relationship, *alone*, can produce even the modest goals of love and work claimed by psychoanalysis; and it is arrogant for human beings to claim unconditional acceptance of clients and to deny there is a similar ability present in this magnificent creation. Where does empathy come from but a loving Power present to all of us who is also more empathetic than any person can be? Secondly, psychotherapy only starts the process of healing; it takes years to produce permanent results from an effective course of psychotherapy. Growth, differentiation, healing, and behavior change are a life-long process. Psychotherapy is the jump-start of this process, not the end of change. If this were so, successful psychotherapy would make people perfectly healthy, differentiated, and sinless. That is obviously untrue.

There are three reasons for using the concept of *experience* as a cornerstone of the philosophical foundation of psychology. First, psychologists often forget that they are using abstractions when theorizing about personality: for example, the Freudian concepts of id, ego, and superego have been reified; i.e., given a material reality like the organs of the heart and lungs. By definition, however, concepts can only approximate reality: they are mere signs pointing to a real experience. This fact allows for much freedom, because many different theories could describe the same experience. For instance, psychoanalysis and Rogerian therapy can be effective in therapy without determining which one is "true." After all, physicists have concluded that light can be described as having both wave and particle properties. This may be the reason why research about the efficacy of psychotherapy in the Florida Studies (Combs, 1969) was not able to identify that any one school was more effective than another was. It only proved that more experienced therapists were better and that some people do better with therapy than without. Theories are a framework for relationship, but the empathetic quality of that relationship is still paramount.[13]

Secondly, the nature of abstraction or thinking about experience removes the person from it. Psychotherapy, however, expects that people will be involved in their relationships. Certainly, therapists and clients must reflect on clients' experience to become aware of the unconscious, automatic, destructive, or dysfunctional relationships; to become aware of how one is behaving is essential to psychotherapy. However, the process of reflection removes the person from relating. The proof of successful psychotherapy is living consciously in healthy relationships with immediacy, not removed from them either through reflection or through automatic patterns learned in the past. Oliver (1977) describes experience as immediate, like a Zen master teaching the art of archery who said, "Bow, arrow, goal and ego, all melt into one another so that I can no longer separate them." (p. 334) In other words, we *are* our thoughts, feelings, and behavior. Moreover, if psychotherapy is successful, we learn to live in today's relationships, not past ones.

Thirdly, thoughts are not truth, despite what Descartes said. Truth is in *being*, not in thought or in striving to follow moral principles. Thoughts remove us from immediacy. Thoughts and written words are signs pointing towards truth. Striving to be moral is the product of self-will alone, not being. The living truth of human relationships has both psychological (learned) and spiritual (teleological) aspects. This truth can be either life-giving or destructive. Any human being has the inherent capacity to be always caring, compassionate, and empathetic, but these qualities are blocked by choices we make and by our experience in relationships. Yet many people express many of these qualities without psychotherapy. However, if we use the guidance of wise thoughts, writings, education, and psychotherapy with the help of a caring and forgiving Higher Power, we become more caring, considerate, compassionate, and empathetic. In other words, we become truly altruistically loving and caring toward self and others. This state is *relationship* or *being the truth*, which can only be attained in relationship with a just, caring, and forgiving Higher Power and cannot be expressed in thoughts or words.

In summary, I have defined a new philosophical basis for psychology on the ontological fundamental of relationality rather than the epistemol-

---

13. This approach to theory is derived from the perspectivism of Bertalanffy (1968).

ogy of knowing and subject/object empiricism. I believe relationality is more consistent with how we are and who we are. My perspective is very consistent with emerging discourse in philosophy and the physical sciences. It has been made clear by numerous thinkers that it is impossible for anyone to be objective. Subjective objectivity or participant/observer concepts describe best what is real. We are products of all our relationships and we can become more loving and caring if we allow ourselves to be freed from the bondage to our past. Psychotherapy can provide one way on the path towards freedom, freedom to choose to be loving unconditionally, at least most of the time. Next I will describe my theistic psychology based on this philosophical foundation, then critique Christian practice and theology.

# 3

# MY CHRISTIAN THEISTIC PSYCHOLOGY

M Y CHRISTIAN THEISTIC PSYCHOLOGY is a contribution to the debate about theistic psychology that emerged at the Fourth Annual Mid-Year Research Conference on Religion and Spirituality at Loyola College in 2006. The debate question was: Is it possible to have a theistic psychology or not? Daniel Helminiak said no; Brent Slife (2006a) said yes.

I chose a theistic worldview over the naturalist one because a theistic worldview reflects the fact that our experience is value-laden. This worldview assumes God is active in many ways in our experience and that sin and forgiveness are part of human experience. The ontological foundation of this worldview is relationality—the inherent relationship of God with each one of us. In a theistic psychology, God is an assumption, just as godlessness is an assumption in the naturalist worldview. Moreover, like Slife (2006a), I acknowledge that God's presence cannot be proven or tested through research any more than the assumptions of the naturalist worldview can be. However, there is a psychological phenomenon that can be the object of research: the Indwelling Spirit. The definition of this phenomenon assumes that God or a Higher Power is the source of its teaching, guiding, healing, and forgiving faculties. A theistic psychology is possible if:

1. It has a viable philosophical rationale.

2. It can produce knowledge through research.

Following are the assumptions of my theistic worldview. It is essential to acknowledge that these assumptions are only mental abstractions in order to avoid the trap of reification. My worldview is an abstraction that only points to reality. It is not real, nor can it ever be. Participating in relationships is the only reality. However, even that statement is an abstraction.

*1. God created the universe and maintains a presence in it to achieve God's ultimate purpose.*

God has an immediate, transcendent, and teleological presence. God has been present to all people and with us as we treat one another, whether we believe it or not. God created this world and the universe where moral values, meaning, and purpose are integral and where sin and evil occur. God maintains a presence in the events of the universe in order to achieve God's will. The universe is inherently teleological and is a presence to off-set the malevolent forces of evil. God does not intervene to stop evil but does chasten or test us, as a parent does a child to help us become unconditionally loving. God loves us unconditionally and wants us to love God, others, the earth, and our society unconditionally—the summary of the law. God tries to guide us to love, but our sin inhibits this guidance until we ask for God's help.

*2. Matter is good and not evil.*

God created the universe as good. The created universe is not an illusion. Matter does not dispose us to sin or evil in and of itself. Matter is morally neutral. The body is not inherently the source of passions and sin simply because it is material. Sin comes from our responses to relationships with self, others, events, God, and our culture.

*3. The ontological assumption of my theistic worldview is relationality.*

All of our experience including our internal experience of ourselves and our experience from conception until today involves relationships. The fundamental of relationality becomes the foundation for spirituality because relationships raise questions such as: What kind of a relationship is it? What is its quality? Is it healthy or unhealthy, life-giving or destructive, hurting oneself or others? The answers lead to descriptions of sin, morality, meaning, and purpose and whether meaning and values are idiosyncratic or universal.

*4. The epistemology of my theistic worldview assumes knowledge is gained through reflection on relationships.*

This assumption is the foundation of theistic psychological research. My theistic psychology is a science that uses research methods based on the assumption that relationality is the foundation of human experience and does not reject the research methods of traditional psychology. This assumption is specifically intended to counteract the subject/object epistemology of the naturalist worldview. Qualitative research methods are essential for research together with quantitative methods because they can elicit the relational aspects of human beings easier than quantitative methods.

*5. Sin and evil are part of the reality for all people.*

I define sin as any attachment, self-belief, or behavior that is destructive to self, others, the earth, or society, or that inhibits the unconditional, loving relationship with God. Sin is evil because it is uncaring, hurtful, unjust, and inhibits the inherent loving nature of human beings. We are disposed to be sinful by our ancestors and parents. Our sin comes from attachments and the way we act them out. These attachments and behavior are the products of relationships and are acted out in relationships. Sin also results from self-centeredness. Malevolent forces work through our attachments and self-centeredness to with the teleological intent to make us miserable, at best, and to destroy us, at worst. No one is inherently evil.

*6. We have the capacity to achieve free will and be altruistic.*

Our free will is either inhibited or paralyzed but is inherently present. Because of our attachments, we are not totally free to choose what is right. However, we can learn to regain our free will learning how we are detached to our internalized images. We can find a way to let go of our attachments to our experience through psychotherapy or other means. When we detach from the destructive images, our will is set free to help us be altruistic and caring and to be thankful for the abundance of love around us, instead of feeling deprived and tormented.

*7. God revealed justice as the way for humans to relate to each other.*

We only know of our relationship with God because God revealed that presence to many people in many ways, both Christian and non-Christian, throughout the centuries. No human being is inherently more important or better than another, even those who are unjust. The principle of loving the just and the unjust supports the assumption that we receive revelations from God because, left to our own devices, we tend to be unjust rather than just. It is irrelevant if we fail at being perfectly just: forgiveness is a quality of God for those who strive to be just. Caring, compassionate justice is the foundation for a healthy society, intimate relationships, and moral behavior. This revelation is supported by Karen Armstrong's study (2006) of religions of the Axial Age, such as Hinduism, Confucianism, Judaism, Daoism, philosophical rationalism in Greece, Buddhism during the period from 900 to 200 BC, and the later flowerings of Judaism in Christianity and Islam. She discovered that these religions share the commonalities of compassion, nonviolence, rejection of egocentrism, abandonment of selfishness, self-criticism, and effective action. This revelation is profound because these religions proclaimed these qualities without initially having any contact with each other. This implies that these values are universal and inherent possibilities for us all if people strive to follow them.

*8. God is the foundation of the psychological phenomenon called the Indwelling Spirit that is inherently present in all people.*

God has an inherent presence in all people to guide, teach, heal, and forgive us and has installed in us the ability to know right from wrong—our conscience. These faculties are not learned but can be inhibited. I assume that God is the foundation for this phenomenon because the Indwelling Spirit unconditionally loves us, as Christian theologians describe God. If it walks like a duck and talks like a duck, it must be a duck. I believe that God would be extremely sadistic to make a covenant with us that expected caring, just, and compassionate relationships, but left us without an immediate presence to help us become caring, just, and compassionate. The Indwelling Spirit is a researchable phenomenon because most people dialogue with themselves about whether they are doing right or wrong. A paradigm statement of this dialogue is, "I knew ____ was wrong, but I did it anyway." Research into this phenomenon can provide valuable knowledge about human experience, healing, and purpose. Much wisdom can be gleaned from paying more attention to the Indwelling Spirit in therapy and research. This concept of God's presence is influenced by the Bible, Christian theology, and psychosynthesis.

Now let me contrast this theistic psychology with the traditions in Christian practice and theology.

# 4

# CRITIQUE OF CHRISTIAN PRACTICE
# AND THEOLOGY

## Limitations of Christian Theology and Teaching

THERE IS ABUNDANT EVIDENCE that both Christian church communities and modern psychotherapy provide healing to people. The churches have had a well-documented tradition of helping people heal and grow spiritually for centuries through pastoral care (Clebsch & Jaekle, 1964). Modern psychology has developed new ways to understand people and help in the healing process. However, as said above, since psychoanalysis was established in this country, spirituality, theology, and religion were anathema in all psychological schools except psychosynthesis and Jungian analysis, until recently. For that reason, many church communities discouraged their members from psychotherapy; some even called it the devil's work. Now is the time for these two disciplines to share their knowledge for the common purpose of healing people. There is no need for any conflict between psychology, spirituality, theology, and Christian religion. Every theology has had an implicit or explicit psychology of human nature. In fact, I believe our culture is now suffering because many clergy and lay people consider psychotherapy more effective at healing even when it has no spiritual orientation.

The legitimate reason for the divorce of modern psychology from Christian spirituality, theology, and religion was to help people who suffered from shame, guilt, unworthiness, unlovability, aggression, addictions, perfectionism, co-dependency, self-criticism, and psychotic disorders that were not being helped by pastoral care methods. Over the centuries, the churches did not address most of these problems effectively, if at all. They became more concerned about morality, orthodoxy, and authority than about listening to people who were suffering from these afflictions, particularly shame and guilt around sexuality. They taught people to use retreats, prayers to saints, good works, and confession to foster healing. These were all healthy, healing spiritual practices, but clergy and pastoral ministers did not recognize how people's past programmed their moral behavior. It was appropriate for clergy to preach about morality, but they did not listen to people: they talked or preached at them. As a result, they missed the source of their suffering.

One good example is the effect of Jansenism on Irish and French-Canadian families. Jansenism was a French mystical movement that Pope Innocent X condemned as heretical in 1653. These teachings were deemed heretical because Cornelius Otto Jansen and his followers taught people they could not follow God's commands without a special grace. Those who received this grace were predetermined to be saved, but people could not be sure if they were predetermined or not. Forgiveness for sins was not a prominent aspect of their teaching: rather, they taught that people were born with inherently evil instincts like sexual urges and aggression, considered sexuality shameful, and encouraged guilt (Cross, 1974, p. 727). These moral teachings were harsh, rigid, and perfectionistic. People had to earn God's love by always striving to follow the One's commandments to the letter. However, because pastoral ministers did not listen to people, it was not recognized that these heretical teachings became the family style of Irish and French-Canadian families. Monica McGoldrick (McGoldrick et al., 1982, pp. 310–37) noted that Jansenism infected Irish families because the priests who went to Ireland in France were trained by Jansenists thereby brought Jansenist moral rigidity back with them. Thus Irish people have a propensity to suffer from shame and guilt, repressed sexuality, and avoid intimacy. Regis Lonelier (McGoldrick et al., 1982, pp. 229–45) described French-Canadian families with very similar traits.

Scrupulosity (the pastoral theology term for perfectionism) was acknowledged as a sin in spiritual direction manuals for many years. Despite that, many Christians believed perfectionism was a legitimate Christian way of life. Until very recently, however, most pastoral ministers were unaware that perfectionism had become a personality style in many people, particularly addicts. Most families in our culture were extremely perfectionistic. Consequently, sin became perverted from its true meaning. Sin was not just about feeling guilty. It meant, "I am a bad person" because I did something wrong. Sin, guilt, and shame became interlocked. Even after confession, people held onto feelings of guilt for being immoral, imperfect, sensual, or sexual. Penitential rites did not relieve people of shame and guilt because the sources of these feelings went unexplored. People were told to stop their compulsive behavior, like Nancy Reagan's *Just Say No to Drugs Campaign*, which is impossible.

The churches did not recognize that human experience (not to be confused with human nature) had changed over the centuries. The law was written on our hearts as our conscience. However, our conscience was inhibited or paralyzed by our idolatrous images, self-destructive behavior, and self-centeredness. Various heretical attitudes became enshrined in people's beliefs about themselves, mostly shame and guilt because of sin. Their personal heresy was actually internalized heresy. Most Christian communities did not recognize that self-criticism and self-hatred were enslaving people and making them selfish and unloving. Because the churches were more concerned about morality, orthodoxy, and author- ity, this personal heresy was not identified as harmful and heretical. The churches did not try to learn, as modern culture has learned, that family dynamics, genetics, and cultural norms can explain the etiology of many behaviors that are appropriately called sin. Ironically, modern psycho- therapy has been a savior for many people from unnecessary suffering.

In reality, most churches lost the true meaning of the Gospel as Good News. What Good News is there in feeling guilt and shame about one's sinful thoughts, such as lusting after a woman as well as adultery, or for just being human? The Good News is that in Christ there is a *new rela- tionship* with God, not a *new law*. Through his resurrection and ascension, we know he is present with us and shares the pains we experience when we become victims of evil and disasters. Christ did not only die once on the cross; Christ now shares the pain and joy of all people through the presence of the Holy Spirit. After all, St. Paul said in 1 Cor 6:19, "You must know your body is the temple of the Holy Spirit." Many people use this passage to convict people of sin, not to guide them towards repentance and forgiveness. God is not only judge of our sinfulness; the One also shares whatever pain or joy we each experience.[1] The Holy Spirit, which is totally connected with the experience of the life, death, resurrection, and ascension of Christ, is present to heal and guide us from our sins. The true

---

1. See my story about God sharing our pain in the "Introduction."

mystery of God is: How is it possible that God is present to all people? Instead of, what are the nature and the mind of God?

The travesty is that these churches and their pastoral ministers have focused too much on sin and God's judgment instead of on this *new relationship* where God is ever present to each of us. They imply that people should stop their sin on their own. They talk about God's forgiveness but do not refer to God's presence as guide and teacher. Some say that God is present mostly to convict people of their sin, instead of the one who *pursues* us to forgive our sin. God is almost never described as sharing in our pain because our bodies are the temples of the Holy Spirit. Most often morality, orthodoxy, and authority are taught as the center of Christian experience, not the Good News of the Gospel. These are truly perfectionistic elements. Some clergy and pastoral ministers forget it is impossible to stop sin without God's help, even when we do our part. They seem to want to *talk at* people, not *listen to* them. If the churches had listened to people instead of preaching and teaching morality, orthodoxy, and authority, they would have heard the pain expressed in shame, pseudoguilt, codependency, perfectionism, and addictions. Thank God for modern psychology starting with Sigmund Freud and twelve-step programs!

## Christian Theology, Symbols, Preaching, and Clinical Theology

I consider the major clinical theology problem suffered by many Christian as well non-Christian clients to be the fracture between crucifixion theology and resurrection theology. The task of theology should be to cement these two events into the cornerstone of our faith, but instead Christian practice and theology have emphasized crucifixion theology over resurrection theology. This overemphasis has seeped into the cultural ethos through Christian influences on cultural institutions and worldview. It has led many people to be preoccupied with sin, self-criticism, and perfectionism. This overemphasis is partly because governmental institutions are based on justice and the rule of law, which was derived from the fundamental principle of justice of the Judeo-Christian tradition. Christian churches maintain this overemphasis through preaching, Christian education, and worship.

Look at our altars and the primary symbol of Christianity! The crucifix, the cross, or icons of the crucifixion are the symbols of our religion. The resurrection is the true foundation of Christianity, but many conservative churches emphasize crucifixion theology over resurrection theology by making pronouncements about sin and morality. The media publish these pronouncements and thereby spread this overemphasis. The churches seldom make public pronouncements about God's loving forgiveness and guidance towards repentance except when telling people God is against homosexuality and abortion. Very few preachers from these churches emphasize the unconditional love of God. I have been lucky enough to find three Roman Catholic parishes where the consistent sermon message is the loving presence of God who guides us from sin.[2] The problem is an obsession with moralizing instead of guiding people to experience the remarkable healing, guidance from sin, and forgiveness that are available from our relationship with Christ in the Holy Spirit of God—the presence of the Risen Lord. In truth, people are encouraged to be preoccupied with sin—the definition of perfectionism.[3] As a consequence, many people become extremely self-critical, self-hating, and perfectionistic while mistakenly believing they are living a true Christian way of life. They focus on their sins and unworthiness of God's love and ignore God's loving acceptance and forgiveness for their sins, because they were taught to do so. I became a victim of the same problem, but it was not through Church teachings. My family was perfectionist because they were victims of the Victorian culture that also suffered from this overemphasis.

Until recently, I believed that the Mass of the Roman Catholic Church did not symbolize the resurrection. However, during a recent sermon[4] I realized that the Mass is a better symbol than any other could be, because it is a ritual embodiment of the life, death, resurrection, ascension, and the Real Presence of Christ with us; it embodies the whole theology of Christ in one event that involves God's presence with living people, not just a remembrance of the past. Hence the Mass, or Eucharist, is the best symbol of the Gospel message, even though it is not a physical one, like the crucifix or an icon, because it is a living symbol, bringing the past

---

2. These parishes are the Paulist Center in Boston, Massachusetts; Our Lady of the Assumption in New Bedford, Massachusetts; and St. Francis Chapel and City Ministry Center and St. Mary's in Providence, Rhode Island. But I had to search far and wide to find these churches.

3. See the section on perfectionism below.

4. This sermon was preached by Father Frank Sevola, OFM, at St. Mary's in Providence, Rhode Island on August 3, 2008.

into the present experience of the faithful. Ironically, since that sermon, I noticed there are statues and paintings of the risen Christ, like the Sacred Heart of Christ, in some Roman Catholic Churches.

There is no inherent theological problem in emphasizing sin or sacrificial love. The problem is the way the Gospel is preached and taught by clergy and pastoral ministers. They overemphasize the importance of the crucifixion, Christ's sacrifice, and sin without mentioning the glories of the resurrection and Christ's presence with us. Most churches ignore this problem except when people talk about scrupulosity in confession or spiritual direction.

The ubiquitous presence of the Cross, the Crucifix, and icons of the crucifixion clearly demonstrate an overemphasis on crucifixion theology. Why did the Church use crosses rather than creating symbols of the resurrection? I believe this happened because the clergy needed to encourage shame and guilt, because they had an unconscious fear that people would shy away from Jesus Christ's sacrifice without promoting the Cross. It seems that preachers are afraid to emphasize resurrection theology because people might be drawn to "warm fuzzy love" and ignore their sin. On one hand, with some justification, clergy fear that people would follow their inner voice without seeking guidance to discern the difference between sin, apostasy, or blasphemy and God's voice. On the other hand, some clergy believe they are the only ones to provide guidance, because they have a special connection with God because of their ordination. Some priests believe Christ only comes to the faithful through the Eucharist. These priests present themselves as the sole distributors of God's presence, because they are the only ones who can transform bread and wine into the body and blood of Christ, and they talk little about Christ's indwelling presence within parishioners. What they do not realize is that emphasizing sin and ignoring Christ's indwelling presence increases sin, not love. People become locked in shame and guilt, divorced from the immediate presence of God's grace, which could guide, teach, and heal them. It literally keeps them *hooked on* or addicted to religion; they have to come to church to get God's grace and then go home alone. The truth is that if people want to be moral, their relationship with a loving God who is always with them will assist them to become more moral and keep them from a death due to sin. Ironically, if clergy and pastoral ministers taught about the indwelling Christ, they would encourage a healthy religious experience, not an addictive one.

This overemphasis on crucifixion theology destroys the Good News of redemption theology. This Good News is that Jesus Christ was the embodiment of God's love and the law. He fulfilled the law by living in a *body* that disposed him to all the temptations we face without being disobedient to God, as Adam was. Yet because he was totally human and not married, Jesus removed procreation as the means to create a nation—the People of God—as was true with Israel where circumcision of the male penis was the sign of the Old Covenant. Faith in Christ in the Holy Spirit of God became the new sign of the People of God, the New Jerusalem for all faithful people, not procreation. He did not submit to the temptation to use his inherent powers to rule over the nation of Israel, because his kingdom was not of this world. His incarnation made it clear that sin was not due to embodiment. Jesus died on the cross for our sins. The cross is the cross of our redemption because the resurrection followed. Crucifixion theology emphasizes morality, the law, sacrifice, obedience to God, and God's unconditional love of us. Resurrection theology, in contrast, emphasizes Christ's triumph over death and sin through the glory of God's love for us, shown by raising Jesus Christ from the dead. Death and our sin have no dominion over us. Jesus Christ showed us it was possible to become like him because he was the embodiment of the law as expressed through his life, death, resurrection, and ascension. Our sin keeps us from being like him. In Christ's resurrection and ascension, the new relationship with God is manifested. This new relationship is an extension of the nature of God described in the Psalms as the one who heals, guides, teaches, forgives sins, and is present with those who follow the commands of God's covenant. In that new relationship, Christ in the Holy Spirit of God is always with us as healer, guide, teacher, and forgiver of sin. The Gospels tell the story of Jesus as healer and the one who loved us so much that he was willing to die for us even though we were sinners. Now with the resurrection and ascension of Christ we can become like him in the fulfillment of the law because he is present with us in our experience. The resurrection theme is the loving presence of God with us to lead us away from slavery to sin—our redemption. This Good News can be an antidote to preoccupation with sin and perfectionism through guidance of spiritual directors and psychotherapists.

These two theologies could be seen as a conflict between the law and God's presence with us, but in truth, there never should be a conflict. These theologies are intrinsically intertwined. Without the resurrection, the crucifixion is meaningless as a way of life. If Jesus had only been crucified, we would probably not know about him or he would be considered a moral teacher at best, as Unitarians believe. However, infinitely more important, without the resurrection we would be left alone to become moral and loving without the help of the indwelling presence of the Risen Christ. We would only have our unaided will to help us. If it were possible to become moral by our own efforts, the Old Covenant would have worked. In essence, we would still be subject to sin. That is what Paul meant by remaining subject to the law. It is obvious that no one should experience a conflict from these theologies in living one's Christian faith. God pursues us to forgive our sins from within and without, that we might repent and become one with God—the *commingling* defined by Irenaeus of Lyon below.

When I realized this problem, I went on a search for a symbol of the resurrection on a trip to Greece. The churches there had many icons. One day on Mykonos, I walked into a small chapel. There it was, an icon of the resurrection—the Anastasis in Greek. I fell to the floor in tears. I could not believe my eyes. Christ was in the center standing on two doors in a cruciform shape above the imprisoned devil, with three prophets on one side and common folk being raised from the dead on the other. At first, I thought Christ was standing on the cross of the crucifixion, but later I learned that in Greek Orthodox iconography, the doors symbolize the crossed doors of hell, not the cross of the crucifixion. However, it is still very significant that the doors are crossed, because this form reminds us that Jesus triumphed over evil and sin on the Cross. Hence, this icon illustrated exactly what I mean by the unity of the crucifixion and the resurrection.

## Early Church Fathers and Overemphasis on Sin

The overemphasis on sin and the law has a long history starting with the writings of the first theologians of the Christian Church, known as the Early Church Fathers. According to Richardson (1969), the patristic period lasted from immediately after New Testament times until the eighth century. When I was a novice at SSJE and later as a student at EDS, I read a series that contained the translations of the writings of the Early Church Fathers (Roberts & Donaldson, 1926) from the first century down to AD 325. Most of them were ascetics and hermits in the desert, or members of early religious orders. Many were bishops who wrote apologetics of the faith against the heresies of the time. In this period, the ascetic life had triumphed over marriage as a preferred Christian lifestyle because asceticism was considered more purely Christian, a higher calling than marriage. In other words, Paul's attitude towards marriage and celibacy became widely accepted as suggested in 1 Cor 7:1, "A man is better off having no relations with a woman." and later when he advised the unmarried and widows, "It would be well if they remain as they are, even as I do myself" (1 Cor 7:8).

All of these writings, with the exception of Irenaeus of Lyon (c. 130– c. 200), were fixated on sin, sacrifice, asceticism, self-mortification, and doing good works. Neither the body nor sex was considered intrinsically evil or sinful, but they were suspect as a potential source of sin because of the power of sexual and aggressive passions. The Church Fathers were ambivalent about how sin and embodiment were related. They took too literally the flesh-versus-the spirit concepts in Paul's writings. They started the tendency in theology to value reason over feelings. Consequently, they had a very negative attitude towards human nature and embodiment. These negative attitudes were also present in Neoplatonic thought, which was inherently dualistic. This dualism seeped into Christian theology because theologians used this philosophy to convey the Christian message. They tried to protect theology from Neoplatonic dualism by saying the body was not the source of sin, but they ended up with ambivalence. In York (1975), I called this dualistic tendency from Neoplatonism the evil aspect of Christian Platonic Theology. This philosophical dualism became a hidden evil in theology because it encouraged ambivalent attitudes towards the sexual and aggressive passions of embodiment. The theologians were unwittingly seduced into ambivalence because they used this philosophy. They were disposed to this ambivalence because they were fixated on the sacrifice of Jesus, his celibacy, and were suspicious of embodiment even though they believed the body was not the source of sin.

In contrast, Irenaeus was more in the tradition of the Johannine writings that emphasized the glorious presence of a God who forgives our sins—a light in the darkness of our sin. He was very affirming of embodiment and human nature because his theology was an apologetic to the Gnostic heretics, who believed the body was the source of sin. He was the only humanistic theologian of that period. His theology was a good example of how theology has the potential to affect feelings and attitudes that people experience, in this case about the body. If his theology had been more widely accepted, people's attitudes towards the body, sexuality, and feelings would be quite different today. However, Origen and Augustine, who were very ambivalent about embodiment and sexuality, later overshadowed his theology.

This early ambivalence towards embodiment led to a culture in western Christianity where joy, feelings, sexuality, and sensual experience became clouded with shame and guilt. Van den Berg (1970) describes this devolution as a cultural phenomenon. He says that western culture had a negative valuation of emotions: they were considered bad and reason good. All sensual pleasures were considered unacceptable as a source of joy. This joyless, sin-obsessed culture lasted until the Renaissance. Van den Berg claims that the Renaissance began when Petrarch looked away to enjoy the gorgeous view while walking up Mt. Ventoux reading Augustine's *Confessions*—although he soon returned to reading Augustine's theology of sin because he felt guilty for enjoying the view. While Petrarch was still vulnerable to the prevailing cultural norms, he is widely considered the father of humanism because his poetry and other writings accepted the expression of feelings.

However, there was a theme in these writings that later got lost—God is the one who transforms us from sinners to saints. Gregory of Nazianzus called this transforming process *theosis*, and Irenaeus called it *commingling*. In this process, God provides the power of transformation. We have to do our part, but sin is not overcome by our own will or charitable acts. We become more caring and loving and less and less sinful as God becomes a part of us. God does not extinguish us; rather, our preoccupation with our self-centeredness is extinguished as the union takes place. This is the true Beatific Vision—union with God from within to without—the experience of transcendent immanency. This unitive process is expressed in contemporary terms by the eleventh step of twelve-step programs: "[We] sought through prayer and meditation to improve our conscious contact with a power greater than ourselves, praying only for knowledge of God's will for us and the power to carry that out." Unfortunately, this truth got lost in Christian theology because of the fixation on sin and sacrifice.

## The Clinical Theology of Perfectionism

This overemphasis on sin and the law has created a culture where many people suffer from perfectionism and often victimize others. Perfectionism is the obsessive, self-critical preoccupation with the need to be always perfect. The rules of perfectionism come from family and cultural norms. Perfectionism torments people because they chronically feel bad when they are not perfect all the time. They are usually depressed, obsessively self-critical, and excessively self-centered. Some people feel guilty even when they make a mistake that is not a moral issue, like a typing error. Some attack others when someone points out a mistake they made. Others are very intolerant of people making mistakes in their work. People are most vulnerable to become perfectionists when parents are unloving, hypercritical, or neglectful.

Perfectionism is a psychotheological problem. The psychological aspect of perfectionism comes from attachment to critical idolatrous images; the theological aspect is the desire always to be perfect from a need to appease the wrath of those godlike idolatrous images or from the belief that God's love needs to be earned. This fear of punishment by the internalized godlike images or God is one characteristic of Jim Fowler's (1978) Stage I: Intuitive-Projective of his stages of faith development. The ages of the children in this stage range from four to seven or eight (p. 42). Hence, perfectionists have never developed beyond this age in their faith development. They are probably fixated at the age when the idolatrous images became internalized. Addicts are prone to perfectionism because their whole history is an attempt to avoid the pain caused by early relationships. Perfectionism has a long history of treatment by spiritual directors and confessors but current psychotherapy treatment has proven to be more effective.

Maria was a client who epitomizes the problem of perfectionism. She was not an addict and her family system did not have any characteristics of addiction. Her father was extremely critical of her, whereas her mother was loving and affectionate. Her self-critical beliefs came from her relationship with her father and her life-giving beliefs from her mother. When she was young, she rejected the church and became a hippie, because she felt plagued by the confusion of sin and self-criticism. After she made many self-critical comments in a session, I gave her a homework assignment to make a list of her self-beliefs. She came to the next session with a short list of life-giving beliefs, but mostly self-critical ones. Some of the life-giving beliefs were: I love my husband. I love my kids. I have a good sense of humor. I am affectionate. Some self-critical beliefs were: I'm very perfectionistic. I hate making mistakes. The glass is always half empty. I'm scared to be passionate in sex. I'm too self-centered. When others are mad, it's my fault. I hate conflict and criticism. Her self-critical beliefs functioned like commandments delivered by a tyrannical god. She believed she had to follow these commandments that tormented her daily. I told her, as I have told others, "If you only lived by the Ten Commandments your life would be infinitely less miserable." As therapy progressed, she began to realize that her perfectionism was not Christian and that she was a spiritual person. She decided to return to attending church.

Many Christians like Maria are unaware that perfectionism is not a Christian way of life. They do not realize that perfectionism actually separates them from the love of God, because they try to become perfect through their own efforts in order to *earn* God's love. They do not believe they are worthy to ask God's help because they are so sinful. They forget that no one can do anything to earn God's love. Perfectionism is an excellent example of *personal heresy*, not Christian theology. It was constructed in relationships with people who were perfectionists like parents or to compensate for feeling, "I am a bad person." Hence, perfectionism is absolutely contrary to the Gospel. It is best characterized as sin because it implies we have to earn God's love. The Gospels and St. Paul make it clear that no one can ever earn God's love. Our sin is too great, no matter how small, to allow us to pay God back for the harm we have caused. God loved us when we were yet sinners. God's love is a gift. In fact, I believe God disposed us to pain in order to make us feel helpless and force us to seek God's help if we desire to be truly loving and good.

Some people interpret the passage in Matthew to mean that Jesus encourages perfection as perfectionists do. "You must be made perfect as your heavenly Father is perfect" (5:48).[5] This interpretation is incorrect because they take this verse out of context and the Greek word translated as *perfect* does not mean perfect. The Greek word, *telos,* means "complete." The preceding passages make clear what Jesus meant by *telos*. Hence, this passage has nothing to do with perfectionism. Jesus says, "My command to you is: love your enemies, pray for your persecutors. This will prove that

---

5. This quote is from *The New American Bible*.

you are sons of your heavenly Father, for his sun rises on the bad and the good, he rains on the just and the unjust" (Matt 5:44–45).[6] Here Jesus was teaching the basic Christian tenet about loving our enemies. He was not talking about the obsessive preoccupation with the sin of perfectionism. In his idea of perfection, everyone is loved, both the good the bad, as God does. God never abandons the unjust, nor should we. *The New English Bible* avoids any reference to perfection by translating Matthew 5:48 as, "There must be no limit to your goodness, as your heavenly Father's goodness knows no bounds."

Burns (1980), a prominent psychologist who treats depression, recognized the spiritual and moral aspects of perfectionists. He said clients believe they are saints when they do something good and sinners when they do not, and he calls it the saint-or-sinner syndrome. They torment themselves with constant self-criticism, and are self-centered and grandiose. Irving Bieber et al., (1962) describe this dynamic as the "inner lawyer." The inner lawyer convicts people of the lesser sin of self-criticism in order to help them avoid the more serious sin of being angry with their parents or others because it would be too threatening to be angry with them. Burns (1980) characterizes perfectionists as having impaired ways of thinking:

- They suffer from black-and-white thinking.
- They fear making mistakes and being criticized, so they try very hard to do everything right.
- They tend to over-generalize; i.e., "I am always wrong."
- They should themselves to death; i.e., "I should have known better" (p. 38).

Driscoll (1982), another psychologist, describes perfectionists as chronic self-critics who try to be good by pulling themselves up by their own bootstraps. They have to punish themselves to get things done right; they feel better if they feel bad. They set goals that are either impossible to attain or when they attain the goal, they move the goal higher. They can never feel good about what they do. His insight into perfectionism

---

6. This is true, but a corollary says that rain falls on the just and the unjust but mostly on the just because the unjust stole the just's umbrella.

justifies why people believe it is a Christian lifestyle: because they suffer so much.

The Hazelden Foundation's *Book of Daily Meditations for Men* (1986) says, "When you can't stand criticism you learn to be a perfectionist" (January 2). This implies that perfectionism is best understood as a defense mechanism. Perfectionists try to keep themselves protected from powerful feelings like shame, unresolved guilt, inadequacy, powerlessness, worthlessness, and fear of criticism. These feelings, sometimes unconscious, are formed from the self-beliefs created by attachment to idolatrous images. Perfectionism is a defense against the punitive power these godlike idolatrous images could unleash on the person.

Psychologists are not the only ones who treat perfectionism; it has a long history of treatment by spiritual directors. They used a very similar concept called *scrupulosity,* which Clebsch and Jaekle (1964) define as, "the client's inability to come to a creative decision as to right or wrong, an inability that is heightened by the fear of sinning no matter that course of action is chosen" (p. 295). They note that, traditionally, confessors would insist that penitents do exactly what the confessor said, even if it violated their conscience. Clebsch and Jaekle believe this treatment made the perfectionism worse because the penitent became dependent on the confessor as the new moral lawgiver. Cross (1974) defines *scrupulosity* with more psychological insight, as the preoccupation with sinning. He notes that it could be the result of believing that self-mortification could overcome sin, but it is more often due to a nervous condition. He also explains that penitents often see sin where there is none, and are usually depressed and self-centered. For example, I know a spiritual director who had a penitent who came to confession many times a month with a long list of sins, usually the same ones. The priest told the penitent that his penance was to come to confession only once a month. This penance and the priest's relationship with this penitent were undoubtedly helpful, but did not address the other characteristics of perfectionism, particularly its profoundly spiritual characteristics:

1. The attempt to earn God's love.
2. The belief that, "I am unworthy of God's love and the love of others because I _____."
3. The attempt to be good by one's own will without asking for God's help.
4. The tendency to hold onto guilt and reject God's forgiveness.

Since perfectionism is not healthy psychologically, theologically, or spiritually, what is the difference between perfectionism and a healthy God-centered spiritual life? The difference is that people become convinced that God loves them even if they are sinful. Perfectionists do not believe this. Those of us, who know we are loved unconditionally, allow God to forgive us and lead us to make amends for our sin. We decide to live a moral life because we are so thankful for unconditional love that we consciously *strive* to please God by doing the things the One expects of us, not just because we fear God's wrath. To support this intention, we regularly assess our behavior through healthy self-examination through some form of confession. A healthy self-examination involves asking, what can I learn from my sin? We ask help from God and others because we know no one can be caring and loving by oneself.

My intention in this section has been to describe the psychological, spiritual, and theological characteristics of perfectionism. In summary, our experience in destructive relationships produces the psychological characteristics of perfectionism. The spiritual characteristic is the way that self-critical beliefs lead people to judge themselves and others, whereas Jesus said, "Pass no judgment, and you will not be judged" (Matt 7:1). The *theological heresy* of perfectionism is the attempt to earn God's love.

Unfortunately, clergy and moral theologians have not developed methods to help people deal with the spiritual and theological heresies of perfectionism. In my mind, it is unconscionable that moral theology has not developed theory or practice to address this problem, which is so clearly a spiritual and theological one. Some moral theologians certainly recognize perfectionism or scrupulosity as a psychological and spiritual problem. However, psychologists are the ones who have developed therapies to cure it. Psychotherapists are the appropriate ones to provide therapy to address the experience in relationships of perfectionists, but confessors and other pastoral ministers need to develop methods to address the spiritual and theological aspects of perfectionism through sermons, Christian education, and pastoral care. It seems that many pastoral ministers have relinquished their healing powers as ministers of God to psychotherapy, just as pastoral counselors abandoned their theological roots to psychology.

## Theology Based on Knowledge from Empirical Sciences

Today's theologians would be much more helpful to Christians and our culture if they used knowledge from current empirical sciences. Traditional theologians, such as the Early Church Fathers, used the philosophies of their day. Their theologies always contained an explicit or implicit psychology of human nature from the thought-world of that era. The philosophies of these theologies did not refer to human experience or attempt to make applications to everyday life. They used unverified reason to make their formulations. However, our contemporary thought–world is based on sciences that use empirical research to verify knowledge. It boggles my mind that most contemporary theologians ignore contemporary psychological, biological, or other scientific knowledge about human nature and the created order. If they used this knowledge, theology would be more consistent with contemporary thought and more related to human experience. All sciences deal with experience in some form because they verify their hypotheses regardless of whether they use a subject/object epistemology or a relational ontology.

Moral theologians are an exception. Medical and sexual ethics demand that contemporary moral theologians use knowledge from the empirical sciences. One example is the moral theology of James Nelson in *Embodiment: an Approach to Sexuality and Christian Theology* (1978). He writes about Christian theology, sexual ethics, and intimacy using contemporary psychological and biological research to develop his ethical theology about sexuality. He develops a sexual theology that affirms our embodiment and our sexual instincts. He describes the negative view of our bodies and feelings contained in most traditional theologies and in the social consciousness. He acknowledges that many people have a dualistic attitude towards their bodies, their feelings, and themselves because of traditional theology. He identifies love and fidelity as the primary principles for his sexual ethics. He recognizes that same-sex relationships can therefore be moral when they are loving and committed.[7] It seems unfortunate to me that Nelson had to learn the psychology of sexuality rather than collaborating with a psychologist. To me, it would make more sense if theologians write about the theological aspect and psychologists write about the psychological aspect of an issue. Such a collaborative

---

7. I use this principle in chapter 7 below.

process would have the advantage of creating a common language, and would maintain the integrity as well as the interconnection of the two disciplines.

Another example of a brilliant use of knowledge from biological, psychological, and other natural sciences to create a contemporary theology is *The Phenomenon of Man* (1959) by Pierre Teilhard de Chardin, SJ. He gained this knowledge from graduate study in theology, geology, and paleontology and from his paleontological fieldwork in China. Teilhard de Chardin said that his book was not a theological essay but a scientific treatise (p. 29). He integrated knowledge from all the sciences to describe how God created a universe where the One is present in matter in some form: a creation with a teleological thrust. The teleology in the evolution of creation is to produce human beings who become united with God. Christ is the principle in creation that leads us to become altruistically loving and compassionate beings. Christian love emerges out of the transforming power of Christ inherently present in the created order. He purposely speaks only of the positive aspects of creation in order to avoid the negativity of the abyss of evil. He does consider evil real but does not elaborate about it. Ironically, his Jesuit Order prohibited him from teaching in France from World War I until after World War II, probably because he used evolution as a central concept, did not write much about evil, and did not mention sin or forgiveness at all. This book profoundly influenced the thinking that led to this one, particularly the concept of the Indwelling Spirit.

In my senior thesis for Episcopal Divinity School (York, 1975), I raised the issue of the need for empirical data in theological reflection:

> In my opinion, a new theology of human nature needs to be developed which takes into account God, embodiment, sin and redemption. The theology should be done with an empirical method which would bring data to the theologians from people in all walks of life and [from] all lifestyles who are struggling to become faithful to Jesus Christ, the Christian Gospel, and a Christian community. (p. 106)

The goal of this thesis was to suggest a method to develop a theology without the ambivalence and suspicion about embodiment, feelings, and sexuality that plagued the Church since the Early Church Fathers. I noted that historically, theologians did not believe that the task of theology was to help the faithful become more loving. Some contemporary notable exceptions were Reinhold Niebuhr (1964), Richard Niebuhr (1972), Gustavo Guiterrez (1973), and Martin Thornton (1972). This new theology would define the faith using contemporary terms and contain a psychology that considers our embodiment and our feelings as blessings even though they can lead us to sin. The task of this theology would be to help people became more loving and compassionate with the help of God and the community. In the thesis, I suggested a project to create this new theology in a parish setting where parishioners participate in theological reflection and apply it to their ministries and their personal lives. This project would be a dialogical theological method. It would include professional theologians and many other specialties that would work together in the planning and would serve as supervisors, organizers, and consultants. The project could not be done by one person or by one specialty. This theology would reflect one important principle learned at EDS: theology should not remain only a cognitive belief, but should become internalized in our consciousness and expressed in our relationships and in ministry. Since then I have recognized that theology needs to be based on human experience in relationship.

Even at that time, I believed that the primary task of theology should be to help people lead a Christian way of life through our relationship with God and the Church, not to create grand philosophical systems. This thesis was my first attempt to define that task by answering the question I asked during sermons at St. John's Bowdoin Street mentioned in the "Introduction," "I believe it is possible to be as loving as you say, but how can I become more loving if you're not helping me?" Further study and reflection led me to suggest a new task for theology.

## A New Task for Theology

The entry for *dogmatic theology*[8] in *The Catholic Encyclopedia* defines theology as "objectively, the science treating God, subjectively, the scientific knowledge of God and Divine things" (p. 1). This traditional notion of theology as a science came from Greek philosophy and persisted in European thought until the Copernican revolution (Richardson, 1969, p. 307). However, this notion of the science of theology is not the one that

---

8. This citation was found on www.newadvent.org/cathen/1450a.htm.

underlies the new task for theology below. Theology can also be a science in the modern sense, if it uses empirical, scientific data and current philosophical notions in theological formulations. Theologians need not fear that scientific research will scrutinize the truths of theology, because theological truths are not natural phenomena; they are assumptions. Empirical science can only research observable phenomena. Hence, a modern notion of theology as a science can be based on the possibility of research to determine the effect of theological doctrines on our moral behavior and our sense of self, and whether theology is internalized or not.

The task of the traditional science of theology was to organize and define the faith about the nature of God in relationship with us and creation. It defined orthodoxy and heresy with no reference to applying this knowledge to everyday life except in moral and pastoral theology. Pastoral theology applied theological and biblical insights to preaching, Christian education, parish ministry, pastoral care, and counseling. However, academic theologians considered pastoral theology an inferior theology because it is not academic enough.

It was called *practical theology*. In seminary, it always struck me as hilarious that pastoral theology was considered *practical theology*, because that meant other theologies were *impractical theology*. I thought systematic theology was indeed impractical theology because it did not describe how to live the faith. Christians were told to believe doctrines. Only moral theology was pastoral. However, these theologians were quick to make moral judgments but were silent about how to internalize fundamental Christian doctrines into moral behavior. They did not define a theory of change for sinful behavior or a theory of conversion such as psychology has. They simply described what was orthodox, heretical, and sinful. In truth, they can be accused of intellectual masturbation. Many theologians spent too much time defining the nature of God and not enough on how God relates to us. Yet theology was mainly about the relationship between God and us. It appeared that many theologians did not believe their theology should help Christians become less sinful and more loving and compassionate, except in pastoral theology.

As mentioned in chapter 3, Karen Armstrong (2006) studied religions of the Axial Age with a similar critique of western theology.[9] Even though they had no initial contact with each other, the sages of

9. The Religions of the Axial Age are listed in section 7 of chapter 3.

these Axial Age religions had a common goal to promote compassion, nonviolence, and selflessness. Their intent was to counter the religious myths and violence of their cultures. The sages of the Axial Age religions had no interest in doctrines, creeds, or metaphysics. She said the English word *belief* was derived from the Middle English word *to love* and the word *creed* was derived from the Latin *cordo* meaning, "I give my heart."[10] For the sages, belief was about doing things, not just assent to creeds. They believed that compassion for all things came before belief. She said that even Rabbinic Judaism did not theologize about monotheism: they were more concerned with living God's Covenant through the law. In contrast, by the eighteenth century in western Christianity, the faith came to mean assent to various creedal statements; leading the faithful to believe that their primary job was to assent to these creeds.

Armstrong decries the tendency to define God because it limits God to our own limited perceptions and does not help us become more compassionate. Buddhists refused to promote theological discussion, because theologizing *prevented* people from experiencing the core of the self that promotes nonviolence, compassion, and selflessness. The Axial Age sages all recognized that God is ineffable and indefinable. Some believed God cannot be described but only *experienced* in silence. The sages believed it was essential to question beliefs and teachings and to test them in personal experience. Today, when Christian theologians and catechists attempt to describe the nature of God, they ignore the insights of these mystics and the author of *The Cloud of Unknowing* (1957), a Christian mystic who writes about the ineffability of God—the God beyond any image of God. Christian theologians and catechists should direct their discourse about the nature of God only toward assisting people to become nonviolent, compassionate, and selfless, not speculate philosophically about the nature of God as the Axial Age sages did. Armstrong made two very important conclusions. First, revelation is not once and for all: it is continuous. When people access their inner wisdom during their spiritual journey, they experience a new revelation because God is made new in them. Secondly, there are many conflicting opinions and creeds in each religion, but the Axial Age sages were consistent in promoting compas-

10. This derivation of *creed* from *cordo* is an unorthodox etymology of the word. Most dictionaries indicate *creed* comes from the Latin word *credo*.

sion, nonviolence, and selflessness, even though their followers did not always follow this wisdom.

I believe western Christian theology has contributed to people's problems rather than helping them. Contemporary psychologies are more effective in assisting people to become more compassionate and selfless than any contemporary theology. Psychotherapists treat clients who have problems caused by excessive moralizing by family, clergy, and church leaders; by theological beliefs, which are totally intellectual instead of guiding people to act with care and love; and by views of the body, sexuality, and feelings that are destructive. Theology has contributed to these problems because:

- It became an academic discipline divorced from helping people live the Gospel.

- It emphasized doctrinal purity.

- It lacks any theory to change sin into moral behavior other than confession, good works, and admonition.

- It has a long history of overemphasis on morality and ambivalence about embodiment.

It seems that the Church has forgotten that Jesus did not call philosophers to be the Twelve Apostles. He called uneducated fishermen: Luke, the physician, and Paul were exceptions. In the Early Church, spreading the Gospel did not depend on the intricacies of any philosophy. In fact, Jesus and Paul specifically warned his disciples against the wisdom of the wise; i.e., the educated. (Matt 11:25, Luke 10:21, 1 Cor 1:19) The dedication of the disciples and Apostles, who told the story of the life, death, and resurrection of Jesus, was sufficient to spread the Gospel. After all, Jesus said, "Whoever does the will of my heavenly father is my brother, my sister, my Mother" (Matt 12:50, Mark 3:35, Luke 8:21). All the apostles and later theologians were always involved with guiding and teaching people about the Gospel. They used empirical methods because they applied their theology to the experience of people who were striving to live the Gospel. They did not sit around in academic settings philosophizing. Many of them were bishops who regularly dealt with the theological, spiritual, parochial, and political problems of their fellow Christians. Contemporary theologians need to do the same. In fact, many of the problems we face today began with the early Church Fathers who integrated Neoplatonic philosophy into Christian theology as discussed above. I swear that this history is a prophetic sign to contemporary theologians: Get back to your roots! You have become puffed up to the stratosphere of esoteric metaphysics and divorced from experience much too long. Beware! A non-Christian psychology has taken your rightful place.

This discussion leads me to propose a new task for theology, which requires theologians:

- To determine if doctrines effect our behavior in relationships through research.

- To use empirical research from contemporary sciences to construct theology, not just research of theological literature.

- To describe the relationship between God and us using contemporary philosophical concepts.

- To empirically test the effect of their theology on moral behavior and self-image of practicing Christians.

- To describe an explicit theory of changing sinful behavior through our relationship with Christ in the Holy Spirit of God and methods to facilitate that change.

- To suggest pastoral implications of their theology.

This task requires an interdisciplinary approach. All theology would have pastoral applications for clergy and laity, not just pastoral theology. Theologians would not just describe doctrines, but would test how those doctrines affect people through empirical research, not to test the truth of doctrines. The object of this research would be to determine how people are affected by this theology, *not* to validate or invalidated the theological truths contained in the doctrines, because "science as such is not concerned with explanation beyond the range of natural phenomena" (Richardson, 1969, p. 308). Theologians would use their own spiritual and relational experience as empirical data in the process of the research. They would have to listen to people, not just write theology. The psychology of this theology should be phenomenological; i.e., based on human experience in relationships and should describe a psychotheology of evil. Hence, the ontological fundamental of the philosophical foundation should be relationality and the epistemology should create data through relational empirical research methods. If they were to determine that a doctrine did not affect how we treat others, this doctrine would be considered pious opinion and not essential for Christians to believe. It seems irrelevant, impractical, and a waste of time for Christians to study theology that simply defines the faith and orthodoxy, but does not help us become more loving, caring, and compassionate. This new task for theology opens up new avenues for psychological and theological research.

A theologian who read the first draft of this chapter criticized the fact that I called this a *new* task for theology; he said Karl Rahner and Bernard Lonergan had already suggested it. However, both of these theologians are so esoteric that few parishioners or clergy could study their theology in order to learn how to become more loving. Esoteric theology implies that the Gospel is esoteric, incomprehensible, and only accessible to the learned few. Theology should have a pastoral component, at the very least, that makes it accessible to the average parishioner through study groups.

Recently, I had an opportunity to discuss these issues with a sincere, intelligent priest. He disagreed with my assumption that systematic theology ought to have a pastoral application. He believed theology is only an academic discipline and does not need to have a pastoral application. It was his job to translate theology into the pastoral theology of preaching, teaching, and pastoral care. He used the analogy of a physician giving him advice about his medical problems. The physician functions as the priest does, interpreting what he learned from academic doctors who write textbooks and then applies that interpretation to his patient's medical problems. What he did not realize was that this analogy actually supports what I am saying. His doctor does apply the knowledge from academic doctors. However, these academics are required to do empirical research and write textbooks *and* treat patients as well. They are not ivory tower philosophers. They do empirical research and practice what they learn and write about with patients. Medicine and psychology are disciplines that use empirical data to help people live more healthy lives and cure diseases; the local physician is not the only one who practices medicine. Christian theology should follow this example: Why should theology be the only discipline in the twenty-first century that does not use empirical research applied to praxis and still call itself a science when the philosophical ethos is empirical science?

A perfect example of how a doctrine can affect our experience and behavior is the doctrine of the Trinity. Trinitarian theology affects who we are and how we behave when we internalize its truth. With our willingness to listen and act, Christ in the Holy Spirit of God transforms us from self-centered sinners to altruistic saints. As we strive to be in relationship with Christ, we become aware that we are not alone in our struggle with suffering and sin. We learn we cannot earn God's love. We begin to love others as ourselves because we are filled with unconditional love even though we continue to sin. If we admit how we have continually subjected ourselves to our idols, and strive to increase our conscious contact with Christ in the Holy Spirit of God, we become transformed more and more into the image of God of our creation. Without this Trinitarian relationship, it is impossible for us to become loving, caring, and kind to others, the creation, and ourselves and be obedient to God. We cannot reach our created potential by our own efforts. We feel forgiven for our sins and let go of unhealthy guilt, shame, negative thinking, and self-centeredness. We treat others with true loving care, not self-destructive caretaking, because we know how much we are loved. In other words, we know and feel we are loved unconditionally even if we sin.

During research for this book, I was astounded to find one study that had all the elements of this new task for theology (Spina, 1979). It was a moral theology study of lesbian relationships described in a doctoral dissertation, which contained empirical data from biological, psychological, and sociological studies. He reviewed the biblical and theological literature on homosexuality from both sides of the issue. He used traditional moral categories to make his conclusions. Spina interviewed lesbians because he believed it is essential for moral theologians to talk with the people about whom they make moral judgments. He used a qualitative research study that included a questionnaire and interviews with a number of lesbians who were single or in partnerships. Unfortunately, he did not detail his empirical research method in the dissertation text because he believed that he had included it. However, he used data from this research throughout the dissertation to guide the development of his argument. He concluded that homosexuality was not a choice and that lesbian relationships were moral if they exhibited fidelity, love, commitment, intimacy, and nonviolence. The last chapter included suggestions for the pastoral ministers who counsel same-sex-oriented people; i.e., a pastoral theology for ministering to them.

# 5

# THE CLINICAL THEOLOGY OF MY CHRISTIAN SPIRITUALITY AND PSYCHOTHERAPY PERSPECTIVE

## Theological Notions and Internalized Images

MY CLINICAL THEOLOGY HAS had a long history of development. My study while I was at the Society of St. John the Evangelist (SSJE) in 1962–63 helped me to feel better about my intelligence and provided the first insights into the relationship between theology, psychology, and a spiritual life. This experience in religious life led to periods of relief from depression and anxiety related to my relationship with my parents and guilt about my sexuality. I learned that a spiritual life in community provided real healing that was better in some ways than my experience in prior psychotherapy. I began to address my issues about a domineering mother and perfectionism with the help of my Father Master, Joseph Upson, SSJE and my confessor, Fr. Patterson, SSJE. When I left, I was convinced that we needed to bring a community spiritual life out of the monastery into everyday life. My study at Episcopal Divinity School (EDS) in the early 1970s taught me that theology and psychology had many commonalities. Yet I already knew that many professional and lay people believed psychology and theology were incompatible. However, I was convinced that psychology can inform theology and theology can inform psychology. My doctoral studies and experience as a psychotherapist raised these questions:

1. How can theology inform psychology and psychology inform theology without eliminating either as a separate discipline?

2. How are sin and addiction related?

3. How can the Christian community support people in conversion from sin and addiction?

One answer to the first question is the *relational self* notion that includes the theological, spiritual, and psychological concepts, described above. Here I explain how the concepts of the relational self can inform the traditional theological concepts of sin, free will, and original sin. In the next chapter, I describe how Trinitarian Theology can influence Christian psychology and psychotherapy through the concept of the Indwelling Spirit.

To review, the relational self refers to our experience in relationships that becomes internalized as images of those relationships. These images become constructs in our neuropsychological program. Our response to these images produces self-belief constructs that in turn program our behavior. The internalized images from life-giving relationships produce life-giving behavior. The self-destructive images produce uncaring and/or abusive behavior to self and others. These self-destructive images become idolized as if they were gods. I call them idolatrous images because they are false gods. Hence, we are guilty of the *sin of idolatry*[1] because these images became more powerful than our love of God and others. These gods are not external idols, made of gold and silver; they are internal. Most of the behavior that acts out these images is also sinful because it is uncaring, demeaning, or abusive toward others or ourselves. For example, if our parents were alcoholics or drug addicts, we either became addicts ourselves and/or developed abusive behaviors towards self or others such as lying, stealing, accepting abusive relationships, low self-esteem, perfectionism, excessive spending, or being irresponsible. If we were called names or beaten, we developed low self-esteem or depression, or became suicidal, and/or abused others in similar ways.

It becomes very clear how powerful this idolatry is when we recall Maria's case, described above. She was abused by family members and other men, refused to forgive herself because she did not tell anyone, and became a prostitute at times and a heavy drug user. She tried many times to stop through treatment in many forms. She loved her children dearly but often relapsed and repeatedly landed in jail. She had given her internalized abuser and her mother ultimate authority over her feelings and behavior, even though part of her knew this was wrong.

---

1. The theological terms are highlighted in *italics*.

This sin of idolatry has similarities with and differences from the traditional Christian concept of sin as described by Richardson (1969), a Protestant source:

> The Christian understanding of sin makes it necessary to distinguish between sin as a state and sins as individual actions. Sin is the prideful state in that man revolts against God and makes himself the measure of all things. . . . Sin's beginning is not when man commits his first unethical act but when he separates himself from God by his unbelief and pride (p. 204).

*The Documents of Vatican II* describes a similar concept of sin:

> [F]rom the very dawn of history man abused his liberty, at the urging of personified Evil. Man set himself against God and sought to find fulfillment apart from God. Although he knew God, he did not glorify Him as God. . . . Examining his heart, man finds that he has inclination towards evil too, and is engulfed by manifold ills that cannot come from his good Creator (p. 211).

The idolatrous images are similar to what Richardson calls "sin as a state," to the Vatican II documents' idea that "man finds that he has inclination towards evil," and to Augustine's concept of concupiscence. Our attachment to these images is the belief that separates us from God: we in truth believe in the false gods instead of God. We gave our power over to these false gods, but no one forced us to do it. Much of who we are and how we act comes from our attachment to these images, which can lead to immoral acts. The internalized images from life-giving relationships and our knowledge of what is loving and right are totally impotent to make our behavior moral because we are attached to or identified with our idolatrous images.

However, the difference between the traditional notion of sin and sin resulting from idolatrous images is that we *did not choose* those relationships. We did not "revolt against God." Our "prideful state" or hedonistic hubris did not lead us to our self-beliefs and attachment to the images. We did not want to separate ourselves from God. We were *victims* of those relationships. That was all we knew. In fact, we were dependent on them and sought love and acceptance from them. Even though we are the ones who constructed ourselves in response to these images, we cannot be blamed for the uncaring, neglectful, or abusive relationships. We are victims of those relationships. When theologians and pastoral ministers say that sin is a "revolt against God" or "a prideful state" or hedonistic desire, they imply that we are responsible for being victims as well as for our sinful attachments and behavior. That description of sin exacerbates shame and guilt. Even though many responses to idolatrous images look like pleasure-seeking addictions, that pleasure-seeking is not *hedonistic*: instead the intention is to anesthetize or to avoid pain. We are trying to blot out the pain of our attachments and our guilt for the things we consider bad. Hence, sin is not pride or revolt against God, as theologians say, but unsuccessful attempts to find God. This explanation is my experience because I always believed in a loving God who dwelt in me, but I acted out sexually for years, was very self-hating, and was attached to the idolatrous images of my parents and my abusers. I sought the pleasure of sex to relieve the pain of my loneliness, the lack of my parents' true love, the lack of loving relationships, and the lack of friends, all of which created a cycle of guilt, anxiety, and depression.

My concept of sin from the idolatrous images does not refer to all sinful acts; it refers to compulsive sin. The sins of idolatry are the result of an inhibited or paralyzed *free will*. These sins are best described as compulsive sin. St. Paul describes compulsive sin very clearly in Rom 7:16: "I cannot even understand my own actions. I do not do what I want to do but what I hate." Also in Rom 7:23–24: "In my inmost self I delight in the law of God, but I perceive that there is . . . a different law, fighting against the law that my reason approves and making me a prisoner under the law . . . the law of sin." Paul is saying that he wanted to do what is right, but his *will* could not stop him from sinning. In other words, he did not have a free will. That sounds like compulsive behavior to me! For us, these sins are the behaviors and thoughts we repeat over and over in our lives. Compulsive sin is a kind of repetition compulsion. These are the sins that confessors hear repeatedly over the years, such as lust, abusive anger, rage, gossip, meanness, promiscuous sexual relationships, gluttony, and perfectionism. We do not want to sin, but we do it anyway.

This concept of compulsive sin raises the question: Do we truly have a free will? The traditional doctrine of free will implies that we can freely choose good over evil at all times, but my understanding of attachments to idolatrous images means that we do not have totally free will. Therefore, the answer to the question is a resounding "No!" With these sins, our will is either compromised or paralyzed. Addicts are the best examples of this common experience: they know that their addiction is wrong, but they do it anyway. It angers me that many theologians and preachers do not understand this common reality. However, the will *is* involved in the choice to turn one's life around through a conversion, or metanoia, by asking for help from a Higher Power and others through twelve-step programs, psychotherapy, or other groups. Theologians and pastoral ministers ought to use these concepts of sin and free will.

Patrick McCormick (1989) identifies compulsive sins that he also calls addictions that do not originate from idolatrous images. They are imposed on us by external cultural systems. These sins originate from attachments that are as powerful as idolatrous images. They include consumerism (materialism), neo-colonialism, militarism (the arms race) and sexism (p. 163). These sins cannot be included in individualistic categories of sin, but they enslave many. Some of us buy into them because we allow ourselves to be victims of the corporate and societal systems that create them. He considers these sins addictive because these systems oppress and control people. They literally hook people, unwittingly. They make promises that cannot be realized, such as "You need many things to be alive"; "The people in poor countries will have prosperity"; "We will have peace if we wage war"; "Women are dependent on men." McCormick says these sins are contained in societal systems. However, our idolatrous images could also be a source of societal sins, because the people who created those images held those views, which would be internalized along with the images. May (1988) lists other attachments that he also calls addictions, such as anger, marriage, memories, revenge, or aversions to airplanes, anger, darkness, germs, birds, food, and the like (pp. 38–39).

There are sins, however, that are not compulsive, such as premeditated murders, many sex crimes, or assaults and murders due to command hallucinations. Premeditated murders and many sex offenses are not compulsive acts, even when the perpetrator repeats them, because perpetrators choose to commit the acts without the conflict of conscience. This conflict is the major difference between compulsive and noncompulsive acts. These perpetrators simply decide to satisfy their selfish needs. These people are like the gangsters who kill as part of their job, those who kill for money, those who kill their spouses out of jealousy, and most sex offenders. They are what Otto Kernberg (1993) calls malignant narcissists. These perpetrators act out a personality disorder, not idolatrous images. They develop this disorder as a result of resentments for trauma that happened to them. They may have had similar experiences to others who do not become perpetrators but they *choose* to hold onto resentments and remain self-centered. Some people decide to be caring and empathetic of others; other people decide to take out their resentments on others. These decisions are not made once, they are made over and over again. The malignant narcissists decide that the world owes them something. Their needs are the most important. They get caught in their resentments and self-centeredness, become bitter and self-absorbed, and do not care about others. Most sex offenders are examples of this narcissism. When I worked at a sex-offender prison, I found it difficult to find inmates who were addicts. I discovered that most of the inmates had no conscience about their offenses and were self-centered malignant narcissists. I could only find a few men who had true guilty consciences about their offenses to form a Sex and Love Addicts Anonymous twelve-step meeting.

Some readers may be surprised that I said murders and assaults due to true mental illness were sinful. These are sinful because they fit my definition of sin; i.e., hurting or abusing self or others. These acts are not compulsive sin because they are the result of a thought disorder, not the person's experience in relationships. However, I believe that those who commit murders and assaults due to mental illness should be imprisoned for the same length of time as those who commit these offenses for other reasons. The mentally ill should not get special treatment for horrendous acts for the same reason all criminals are imprisoned—to punish them and to send a message that criminal acts are illegal and/or immoral. The difference would be where the mentally ill are imprisoned: a prison mental hospital is the more appropriate place for mentally ill offenders than the prisons for all other offenders.

However, it is important to acknowledge that idolatrous images are not the only source of sinful acts. All of us commit sins that are non-compulsive for selfish reasons, very similar to the malignant narcissists. We steal from our workplace, lie on our income taxes, cheat on tests to get ahead, rage while driving, and commit many other selfish acts. We too have no empathy for how our behavior affects others. These sins are *freely chosen* to satisfy selfish needs that are independent of idolatrous images but are not due to a personality disorder. These choices do involve a *free will*.

I define *sin* as:

1. The attachment to idolatrous images.

2. Any behavior that is uncaring, harmful, destructive, demeaning, injurious, or abusive to self, others, the earth, and the social order.

These attachments and behaviors separate us from experiencing the incarnate presence of God. We are not responsible for the idolatrous images, which are internalized, but we are responsible for our attachments to these images, which produce our sin and keep us enslaved. Our compulsive sin acts out these images as immoral and self-demeaning behavior such as stealing, raging, and selfishness. The self-demeaning acts are attitudes and behavior like invading others' boundaries, ego inflation, being overly responsible, being hypersensitive to criticism or rejection, and perfectionism (Whitefield, 1991, p. 56). Claudia Black (1981), Melody Beattie (1987), and Janet Woititz (1983) describe co-dependency, adult children of alcoholics (ACOA), or dysfunctional families, and list similar behaviors and attitudes in books.

It may be surprising to some readers that I consider these ACOA characteristics and attitudes sinful. I consider them sinful because they destroy healthy self-love and contribute to separating us from the presence of God and choosing to do God's will. I appear to add insult to injury to say these behaviors are sinful, but if individuals do not know they are hurting themselves, they will never change. The issue for psychotherapists is how to tell people that they are being self-injurious without being judgmental: calling an act a sin does not necessarily create shame and guilt.

Some readers are probably wondering why I include self-hatred as a sin; it seems as if I am simply adding one more thing to feel guilty and ashamed of. Two points are relevant here. First, self-hatred is a form of guilt and shame, so I am not adding any new moral category. Secondly, self-hatred causes people to suffer, both self and others. It is a form of depression. Self-hatred is self-destructive and, therefore, a sin in my definition. It is as important to confess self-hatred as any other sin because confessing it reminds us that we do not have to be subject to it and that we do not deserve to be self-hating.

This concept of compulsive sin suggests that the theological doctrine of free will needs to be modified. The traditional doctrine implies we have the freedom to choose good over evil freely at all times, but the concept of compulsive sin means that we do not have total free will. St. Paul said as much. In fact, if we all had free will, there would be much less sin. Our will is inhibited at best and paralyzed at worst, because we have given our idolatrous images ultimate power. These images inhibit our free will because our needs for love and caring went unsatisfied and we compulsively seek to satisfy those needs. In fact, we will have no truly free will until we free ourselves from the idolatrous images with the help of our Higher Power and others. In contrast, our life-giving images from caring and loving relationships do not inhibit our free will, because our needs for love and caring *were* satisfied.

Gerald May (1988) says our will is a *split will*, not a free will, and also bases this concept on St. Paul's statement in Romans 7:16, quoted above. He says we have the will to do what is right, but we find ourselves powerless to stop the sinful behavior much of the time. He considers what I call compulsive sin, addiction. Addicts are the clearest examples of this split will. I often say to my addicted clients, "If all people had free will, there would be no addicts in the world." Everyone would choose to do what is right. No one chooses to become an addict; it occurs over many experiences and circumstances. The problem is that the will of addicts is impaired or paralyzed because they need to anesthetize their responses to the idolatrous images, their intense feelings from the trauma of past abusive experiences, and the guilt and shame about their own behavior. The addiction is an unconscious solution to the past trauma. They know what is right, but they cannot do it. However, addicts can regain their free will if they discover the unconscious motivations to their addiction. They become released from slavery to past relationships, the attachment to their idolatrous images, and the resulting addictive behavior. The doctrine of free will needs to be modified to reflect the truth of the split will and to suggest an effective method to free the will from bondage. All compulsive sin can be described and overcome using this model.

One of the most fascinating discoveries made by Merle Jordan was that some people seek various ways to make *atonement* for their attachment to their idolatrous images. They unconsciously try to compensate for perceived or real sins, failings, guilt, or pseudoguilt. This atonement is not related to Christ's atonement for our sins in any way; it is *self-atonement*. Many people seek to earn the love of others or God by always striving to be right and good. They feel shame and guilt for what they did wrong, but never accept forgiveness for their sinful behavior. They compensate by doing self-sacrificing good works that look like altruism. They become people-pleasers because they are trying to appease the internalized images of parents and/or others who they fear would punish them for their sins: they unconsciously fear the wrath of their idolatrous images. Some believe that if they do what others want, these people will become the caring, loving people they always wanted. Sometimes they do not believe they can be loved as they are and are usually self-hating. Sometimes they believe they are fundamentally unworthy of anything good happening to them. Some of them enable addicts and/or they become addicts of one sort or another. Some of them cannot forgive themselves for things they did that are wrong. Some of them strive to be perfect by their own efforts or give up altogether. They hurt others by being mean because they were hurt. Self-atonement has clear perfectionist and codependent elements.

Jim is an excellent example of self-atonement, and he is Jewish. This client was a victim of a father who was overpowering, verbally humiliating, and threatening. Many family members had anxiety disorders, but his panic disorder was exacerbated by this trauma history. He believed he was being a caring person when he always did what people asked him to do, no matter what the request. He felt he was a bad person as his father said. Jim felt guilty because he sometimes acted like his father and had stolen money from a relative. He did not want to hurt someone's feelings by saying "no." He often drove a friend who was a heroin addict to get drugs. Another acquaintance asked Jim for $5,500 to buy a car, and he gave it to him. In therapy, it became clear that he believed he needed to buy friends. Jim was not worthy of self-respect because his father mistreated him. He could not be angry with anyone without having a panic attack. He believed he had no rights to his anger or being self-protective because he would be attacked or worse if he acted like his father. He did not know the difference between selfishness and self-affirmation. Jim's personal heresy consisted of feeling unworthy of friends unless he bought them in some way or did what they wanted. His generosity was self-defeating, not self-loving. He hated himself and had low self-esteem. He could never trust his own opinions or feelings, particularly anger. Experiencing these feelings often led to panic attacks in current relationships.

These characteristics of self-atonement create a personal heresy for the person that is totally contrary to the saving Grace of Jesus Christ. Self-atonement is a second form of idolatry because people use self-destructive ways to compensate for their shame and sinful behavior, as

Jim did, without asking God or anyone to help. No matter how hard we try, we cannot make God love us. We cannot earn God's love: God gives love freely. Even though we sin, God loves us. The true compensation for our sin is loving our enemies, including our abusers, because Jesus calls us to pray for our enemies. All attempts at self-atonement are self-defeating, personal theological heresies, and false Christian theology.

This etiology of sin from idolatrous images can also clarify the theological notion of *original sin* for today's Christians. The question is: What is original sin in terms of contemporary psychological concepts? According to Richardson (1969), St. Augustine believed original sin was transmitted through procreation. That means that we inherit guilt and are disposed to sin. He also says that contemporary theologians do not believe we inherit guilt, but acknowledge that we do not follow God's will and purpose (p. 204). This understanding of original sin does not take into account the contemporary research about nature and nurture. Jean-Jacques Rousseau (1712–1778) believed that children were born virtuous and became corrupted by society. In contrast, current research and theories suggest that children can both be egocentric and have the capacity to be empathetic. Baldwin (Broughton & Freeman-Moir, 1982), Piaget (1967), Kolberg (1972), and Fowler (1978) construct theories of development based on research that indicates there are both genetic and experiential components to our development from egocentric to other-centric beings. Winnicott (1960) describes infants after birth as undifferentiated from their mothers. Infants are the center of their world. Whatever the mother feels, the infant feels. Infants slowly differentiate from the mother as they develop. This theory appears to indicate that both self-centeredness and other-centeredness are inherent; i.e., the propensity for self-centered sin as well as the inherent ability to love. Other research demonstrates that some destructive behaviors have a genetic predisposition such as alcoholism (Buck 1998) and aggression (Nelson 2006). The destructive behaviors in bipolar disorders, anxiety disorders, or schizophrenics also have genetic links (Hindmarch 2002). However, the destructive behavior from idolatrous images is definitely the product of our experience in relationships (nurture) starting with conception. These behaviors are transmitted relationally, not biologically. In sum, research demonstrates that genetics (nature) and experience in relationships (nurture) both influence destructive behavior.

Frankly, the nature and nurture aspects of original sin are common sense. No parents are completely loving. Many of us were abused by others. Calamities, deaths, and sickness occurred that contributed to our idolatrous images and sinful behavior. We all are self-centered beings regardless of whether we were born that way or not. We were not completely loved and cared for, nor were our parents, nor were their parents, all the way back to the beginning of the human race. In this sense, I believe original sin is comprised of theological, psychological, and genetic components. We are not to blame for our propensity to sin. We have a propensity to sin because God created a world where sin was possible because of genetic inheritance, human choice, idolatrous self-beliefs, and self-centeredness. We were born into a world where no one is completely caring and loving. Events occurred that hurt most of us in some way. We internalized images from all of our relationships. We became attached to them and we acted them out. We do not always follow God's will and purpose, but God wants us to be caring and loving of each other and our enemies. God has placed his presence in us to guide us to his will for us—our Indwelling Spirit. Therefore, guilt is not inherited as Augustine thought; although, there is evidence that some destructive behaviors are linked to genes that are inherited. In theological and biblical terms, the sins of the "fathers" (parents and others) are passed on to the children. In psychological terms, then, sin is the result of nature (genetics) and nurture (experience in relationships).

Please do not think I am implying that we are not responsible for our sin. We are *not* responsible for those who victimized us, but we *are* responsible for our response to them that led to sin. We were the ones who constructed our particular reactions to the idolatrous images with sinful beliefs and acts. These sins became our solutions to the problems created by those relationships that were internalized. *Our* response to these relationships created the behavior; no one else did. We constructed our own reality and we can deconstruct it. Our idolatrous images are our reality; that is our truth. This means that we are responsible for our sinful behavior at any age it occurs. For example, if we hit someone at two-years old because our parents hit us, or have sex with someone at seven-years old because we are desperate for love, we cannot excuse that behavior. We performed the act, no one else did. Neither our parents, nor our abusers, nor the devil made us do it. We did it. It is understandable where our behavior comes from, but *we* are responsible for how we act.

I do not believe, however, that it is sufficient to describe the Christian doctrine of original sin without saying how to be released from its bondage. Almost all of us are some combination of sinful and loving beings. Our experience in relationships and our Indwelling Spirit provide us with loving parts as well as sinful ones. As children, we did not love ourselves, others, and God, unconditionally. Nevertheless, if we respond to the guidance of our Indwelling Spirit, we can become unconditionally loving. Baptism is the sacrament that immerses us in the incarnation, death, resurrection and ascension of Christ and makes us members of the Christian community and the community of caring people; thereby we are not left alone on this journey. We can use psychotherapy, spiritual direction, our Indwelling Spirit, and loving, supportive relationships from within the Christian community and outside to guide and help us along our way. We cannot earn God's love by self-atonement, but we do need to make amends for our sin, at the very least by acting differently. We can learn to love and forgive our enemies and our abusers. To paraphrase St. Paul, our life-giving behavior is living by the Spirit and our self-destructive behavior is living by the flesh. This process is similar to Freud's goals of psychoanalysis—to love and to work—but these goals are achieved by a new relationship with God and with others, not by "ego" replacing "id." Spiritually and theologically, this process is the unfolding of complete love from within and without. Psychotherapy facilitates the release from the bondage of sin by helping us detach from the internalized images.

## The Anatomy of Sin

At the time I was writing this section, I had a session with a Nadine who was having an affair with a man. She was living with another man whom she married. The affair started before the marriage. In the past, she was promiscuous and was molested. She knew she was a sex and love addict and went to a few Sex and Love Addicts Anonymous meetings but had not acted out sexually for years until this affair. In past sessions, I had restrained myself from telling her that her behavior was wrong, but reminded her that she was running the risk of destroying her marriage. In one session, it dawned on me why it was important not to say her adultery was wrong. As she visualized being with both men, I asked her, "What keeps you in the affair when you know the sex with him is not that good and you know what could happen to your marriage?" After a short silence, she answered, "Because I'm angry with my husband."

Not judging her adultery as immoral had two very important outcomes. First, if I judged her, she would probably have felt more shame, guilt, judgment, and anger and would probably have continued the affair anyway. Second, if I had not asked her what kept her stuck in the affair, she would never have found the unconscious motivation. She had no idea that she was afraid to get angry with her husband because she lived with the fear that he would abandon her as her parents did. She had grown up in a family where she was neglected emotionally by both parents. She avoided conflict at all costs. She feared that she would lose any relationship if she got angry. That experience taught me very clearly why it is important to understand the motivation and etiology of immoral behavior instead of judging it. Now she had the potential to choose freely to change her behavior since she had learned her unconscious motivation to avoid anger. She decided to stop the affair at the next session. She had also expressed her anger directly with her husband a few times between sessions and risked asking him if her fears of him abandoning her were true.

This client's discovery of the unconscious motivation and etiology of her adultery is an example of what I call *the anatomy of sin*. This term refers to identifying the etiology and unconscious motivation for sinful behavior through psychotherapy and research studies. I have already defined sin as attachments to idolatrous images or other attachments that are acted out as uncaring, harmful, destructive, demeaning, injurious, or abusive behavior towards self, others, the earth, or the social order. Psychologists have studied the etiology of many destructive behaviors through research and in clients in psychotherapy in order to develop various psychotherapies to overcome bondage to those behaviors. My purpose for describing the anatomy of sin is to provide psychotherapists, theologians, and clergy with the same language to help people in the process of overcoming the bondage to sinful destructive behavior.

Let me describe a number of examples of the anatomy of some sins. Remember Maria? She is an example of someone who could not give up her guilty due to the sin of attachment to idolatrous images and the behavior that acts them out. She was physically and emotionally abused by her parents and sexually abused by family members. She became attached to the internalized images and acted them out by becoming a prostitute and a drug addict, neglecting her own children by going to jail. Her addiction was an attempt to stop the pain of past abuse and overpowering guilt. She sought God in her addictions. Yet she had difficulty forgiving herself for the abuse. Unconsciously, she believed she was unworthy of God's love. She often relapsed in treatment and went to jail, because she could not let go of her guilt.

Jane also had a sexual abuse past and became a drug addict. She was given to men by her mother as a sex object and witnessed a murder. Her mother also left her with physically and emotionally abusive bikers. She acted out her attachment to the internalized images of these relationships because Jane believed she was alone in the world and had to fend for herself. The memories of past trauma led her to various addictions in order to stop the pain. She also developed a psychotic depression and was often hospitalized because she heard command voices to hurt herself by various means. It is unclear whether the command voices were a true mental illness or a borderline personality disorder caused by a horrendous childhood. Jane's sins were the attachment to the idolatrous images from the traumatic relationships and the behavior that acted them out. Her history of drug addiction was an attempt to cope with her horrific past and self-hatred. Her suicidal attempts were a desire to blot out the past.

Victims of sexual, emotional, or physical abuse are good examples of the motivation of the anatomy of sin. Professionals in the field have observed that some sexual predators choose children of the age at which they were abused, and some physically abused people become domestic violence perpetrators. Yet some victims of sexual and physical abuse do not perpetrate on anyone, although they usually develop other destructive behaviors. Some become sex and relationship addicts. They compulsively act out sexually in various ways and/or seek abusive relationships (Carnes, 1983). Norwood (1985) tells stories of many women from dysfunctional families and victims of abuse who became involved in serial monogamy, promiscuous behavior, prostitution, and abusive relationships. Sex and love addicts are usually self-critical, sometimes suicidal, and often mean to others in some way. Patrick Carnes (1989) has done research that indicates that 80 percent of sex addicts say they were abused sexually or physically as children. It is clear that the sins of addicts are abusing self and others, and attachment to idolatrous images.

Jim's[2] experience of horrific verbal abuse from his father was just as debilitating to him as physically or sexually abuse would have been. Throughout his childhood, his father would humiliate, threaten, and yell at him for anything his father considered wrong. He believed he could not question his father or get angry with him. His father would call him names such as "cunt" and "wimp" and tell him that he was never going to amount to anything. Jim felt paralyzed and could not leave the room for fear of more abuse. His mother and sister were also verbally abused, but he was more severely targeted because his father did not want a second son. His mother did not protect him from his father, either. He developed a chronic panic disorder that worsened over the years to the point where he quit work and went on disability. He was probably genetically disposed to develop severe anxiety, as other family members also had panic orders, but his anxiety also had a clear psychological component. He became extremely anxious when he was in the back of stores or in a doctor's office away from an exit. He had generalized his experience of being paralyzed when yelled at by his father. He used to abuse alcohol and occasionally had sex with abusive straight men. His friends often told him that he was acting like his father. He sometimes became verbally abusive, mean, angry, and controlling. His major sin was holding onto his idolatrous image of his father, which was expressed in panic attacks. In early sessions in therapy, he was petrified of getting angry with his father, even in my office. After a session where he expressed some anger towards his father, he had a dream that he hit his father with a baseball bat. It appeared that the unconscious motivation to keep attached to his idolatrous image was the fear of becoming engulfed in homicidal rage at his father. He has sacrificed himself to a life of anxiety and panic attacks to prevent him from releasing uncontrollable explosive rage at the least and murderous rage at the worst. However, sometime later he was able to be appropriately angry with his father without guilt.

Jim's anxiety disorder is not his sin. His sin is acting out his attachment to the idolatrous image of his father that exacerbated his anxiety disorder. This attachment makes him miserable most of the time and sometimes hurts others. This attachment is acted out as beliefs that he has no right to be appropriately angry, no right to his own opinions, and low

---

2. Jim was the one described above in the description of *self-atonement* who had to buy friends.

self-esteem. His sinful behavior is drug and alcohol abuse, promiscuous sex, buying friends by giving them money or whatever they asked for, self-hatred, and self-atoning behavior. His work in therapy is relieving him from much of the bondage to his anxiety disorder.

The process of identifying the etiology of sinful destructive behavior through psychotherapy has been very helpful, but it also has some limitations. Psychotherapists started the process of identifying the etiology of destructive behavior because they did not want to moralize with clients as some clergy and theologians did. It became obvious to them that telling clients that behavior was wrong, or to stop it, did not change it. Psychotherapists learned long ago that no one can be heal or released from the power of destructive behavior unless one knows the unconscious motivation and etiology of that behavior. They realized that telling people to stop destructive behavior or saying it was wrong only increased guilt and shame and inhibited the process of change in therapy. Early psychoanalysts and other psychotherapists never used the word *sin,* but they guided clients to realize that their behavior was destructive. These professionals did know, however, that having clients share their guilty feelings was essential. This sharing is a form of confession. Clergy and psychotherapists know that confession has the potential of relieving the person of shame and guilt, although they also know that some people hold onto their guilt and shame.

Unfortunately, in the attempt to determine the etiology of behavior, psychotherapists were accused of letting clients disown responsibility for destructive behavior. As I said above, psychoanalysts did not make any value judgments about behavior, until recently. Most psychoanalysts considered behavior amoral, particularly sexual behaviors. Psychotherapists were accused of excusing destructive behavior or being amoral about it. I have heard stories from people who were unconcerned about how they hurt others because their therapist was trying to help them *express* themselves, without assisting them to learn how their behavior might affect someone else. This problem was epitomized in the Sergeant Krupke song from *West Side Story* of the 1950s. The scene of this song was a mock trial of the police officer for arresting other gang members. The "judge" says that these young men are not juvenile delinquents; rather they are psychologically sick because they come from dysfunctional homes riddled with alcoholism and drug addiction. He says they need psychoanalysis, not jail. The "judge" excuses their behavior because they did not have enough love, just as the psychoanalysts of that day said. He identified the etiology of the behavior, but relieved them of responsibility for their actions. I do not agree with this "judge," however. It is important to understand the etiology of harmful behavior, but that does not excuse anyone from taking responsibility for harming self or others, which I judge to be *sin,* a moral judgment.

I made an exception to the rule of being nonjudgmental of destructive behavior when I was working with sex offenders. I told the ones who were not sex addicts that their behavior was wrong because they had no clue how much they hurt their victims. They did not have a guilty conscience because their denial was so strong. Domestic violence perpetrators also need to be told that their behavior is wrong for the same reason. The most successful treatment for these clients has been teaching empathy for their victims in order to help them to develop a guilty conscience. Sex offenders and domestic violence perpetrators are on the malignant narcissism end of the narcissistic continuum of Kernberg (1993). Hence, they are so fixated on satisfying their own needs that they have no empathy for how their behavior affects their victims. They can develop a conscience and empathy if they learn that their behavior has consequences. Hopefully, their jail experience and treatment will help them realize how much pain they cause their victims.

I treat other clients differently. Some clients already know that their thoughts, feelings, and behavior are sinful because they are spiritual or religious people. I affirm that they should feel guilty if they hurt someone or themselves but I do not want to relieve them of healthy shame. Healthy shame helps people avoid repeating sinful behavior. However, it is time to let the guilt go, not hold onto it. I ask these clients, "How do you get a jackass's attention? Hit him over the head with a two-by-four. Your guilt is like the two-by-four. The purpose of guilt is to get your attention and that is all it's good for. It's time to let it go." Unfortunately, self-forgiveness is *the* most difficult problem for many clients. Many clients hold onto their shame and guilt because they believe that they did something wrong and need to punish themselves. They do not realize that all of us sin in some way and can be forgiven. To sin is a part of being human. If they learn how they reinforce the guilt and shame in current relationships and in their attachments, they learn to let it go. This process is a task for psychotherapy and spiritual direction.

Here I have provided a few examples of the anatomy of sin in order to explain what I meant by it. I did not intend to do an exhaustive study of the etiology of sin. Many research studies could describe this etiology. My intention was to give examples of the anatomy of sin to demonstrate that psychologists, theologians, and clergy could use the same language to help us overcome our bondage to sin. Some readers may be surprised that I included addictions in the list of sins above. However, remember, I define sin as any behavior, belief, or attachment that is hurtful, destructive, or uncaring. Addictions are certainly hurtful, destructive, and uncaring toward addicts and the people around them. They are paradigmatic examples of compulsive sins, where the will is compromised or paralyzed. As I have explained, compulsive sin is not a decision of the will to be destructive; it is automatic behavior. Compulsive sins are the result of attachments and beliefs that overpower the will in its desire to be moral. Addictions are compulsive behaviors by definition. Sin and addiction is the subject of the next section.

**Sin as Addiction; Addiction as Sin.**

The first inspiration for sin as addiction came from Krister Stendahl (1976) in his speech to the APA in 1961, "The Apostle Paul and the Introspective Conscience of the West." His analysis of Romans 7:15–16 made it clear that Paul was describing *compulsive sin*, as discussed above, not a guilty conscience. "I cannot even understand my own actions. I do not do what I want to do but what I hate." This passage sounded like compulsive sin or addiction to me. Just like an addict, Paul knew what was right but sinned anyway. His will was enslaved to the power of sin that he believed came from "the flesh." In Romans 7:14, he said, "I am weak flesh sold into slavery to sin." Addicts can be described as enslaved to their addiction and the motivations behind it. By definition, they know it is not good for them to eat, drink, spend money, drug, gamble, or have sex compulsively, but they do it any way.

Both McCormick (1989) and May (1988) refer to this Romans passage to conclude that sin is addiction and addiction is sin. McCormick describes how the various traditional models of sin—defilement, punishment, and crime—have serious defects (p. 72). Instead, he describes the disease model of sin and addiction as a compassionate way to deal with sin. Yet he makes clear that we are responsible for our destructive sinful acts. May believes that the psychological, physical, and spiritual dynamics of addiction are alive in every person and lead to addiction to ideas, work, or power (p. 3). He goes so far as to say that all of us can be called addicts because some of our behavior works the way alcoholism and drug addictions do (p. 11). He provides a long list of "attraction addictions" such as approval, attractiveness, pets, popcorn, and television, and "aversion addictions" such as anger, airplanes, animals, and disapproval. He makes the point that some addictions are more destructive than others are but no addictions are good, because "they impede human freedom and diminish the human spirit" (p. 39).[3]

My major point is that in compulsive sin, the will is compromised or paralyzed. It is impossible for us to make free moral choices. The compulsivity of sin overpowers what we know is right. Therefore, it is more truthful to call compulsive sin an addiction. Even those who sin by a moral choice argue with themselves whether their act is right or wrong, unless they are malignant narcissists. By calling sin addiction, the disease model replaces the defilement, punishment, and crime models for sin (McCormick, 1989). The disease model makes it clear that we did not choose to be disposed to sin but are responsible for dealing with how we hurt self, others, the earth, society, and our relationship with God. This model encourages us to ask for help from God and others in order to relieve us of our slavery to sin. Hence, grace and compassion are inherent elements in the disease model of sin, unlike in the other models. The disease model also helps us remove the sting of self-destructive shame and guides us to value healthy shame. Self-destructive shame such as, "I am bad because I am an addict," leads to more addictive behavior. Nevertheless, healthy shame, such as feeling ashamed for stealing from the family or losing the house to the bank because of gambling, helps us remember the consequences of our addiction in order to stay clean and sober. In short, the disease model of sin is less judgmental and punitive and more therapeutic. Conversely, if we define addictions as sin, we acknowledge the reality that there is no difference in psychological, neurological, and spiritual processes between tradition-

---

3. Some readers may think May is overextending the paradigm of addictions, but he makes it clear that many behaviors and feelings are compulsive and destructive to healthy self-images and relationships. His list is similar to the traditional moral theology categories of venial and mortal sins: the mortal sins are the life-debilitating addictions, such as drug, alcohol, sex, and gambling; whereas those listed as "attraction addictions" and "aversive addictions" are the venial sins.

ally defined addictions and traditionally defined sins. The disease model is more humanistic and easily understood. It applies profound spiritual, psychological, and medical concepts to everyday experience. The punishment, defilement, and criminal models are infused with esoteric philosophies devoid of experiential concepts. Also, the need to take responsibility for our addictions is made much clearer.

During Ronald Reagan's presidency, his wife Nancy Reagan championed the slogan, "Just Say No to Drugs." That slogan may help those who never used drugs, but it could never help addicts: they have lost the ability to say no. As I said, a paralyzed or inhibited will is the major hallmark of addiction. However, it is possible and essential for addicts to take responsibility for how their addiction has hurt them and others. They need to do everything in their power to get help to turn their life around by using psychotherapy, spiritual direction, and/or twelve-step programs. They cannot stop the compulsive behavior on their own. That is what the first step of all twelve-step programs means. They did not become addicts by themselves and they will not be relieved of the slavery to the addiction alone, either. Twelve-step programs were designed to help in this process.

AA and other addict groups employed the disease model in creating the twelve-step program movement. These programs are designed to help addicts stop their addictive behavior and take responsibility for it by participating in a supportive community with people who have similar problems. Paradoxically, the program teaches addicts that they are powerless over their addiction and their lives have become unmanageable, but that it is possible to stop the addictive behavior, if they ask for help from others. Their *will, on their own,* cannot stop the addiction. They did not choose to become addicts, but they *are* now responsible for doing something about their destructive behavior. They formed their addiction in relationships, so they cannot stop their addictive behavior. They need to develop healthy, caring, loving relationships with people who will support them unlike those who did not in their earlier lives. Using my terms, their attachment to idolatrous images is replaced by experience with caring, unconditionally loving relationships with others and God. They are released from their attachments by confessing what they have done to themselves and others, the good as well as the bad. Twelve-step-program literature helps in the recovery process because it is replete with references to the Higher Power as an indwelling presence. Therefore, it is possible to be released from the slavery to these idolatrous images with the help of others and a relationship with some form of Higher Power. However, because addictions and idolatrous images are contained in a neuropsychological program that affects brain biochemistry, we are always vulnerable to relapse and sin. We can be released from the captivity of sin, but we are never totally free of sin, at least most of us. It appears that God left us with this vulnerability to help us know we cannot live without God. This vulnerability is like St. Paul's "thorn in the flesh" (2 Cor 12:7). In other words, we will always sin in some way.

## The Etiology of Sin and Church Teaching

My primary purpose for addressing the theological concepts of sin, original sin, and free will is to challenge theologians and the Roman Catholic Magisterium to use modern psychological concepts to formulate theology. I do not reject traditional theology about sin, original sin, free will, or atonement. However, modern psychology has learned a great deal that could inform these concepts for today's world. Historically, theology has always had an implicit or explicit psychology that reflected the psychological worldview of the day. Contemporary psychological concepts can be used if theologians and psychologists agree on a common language and worldview. One possibility is to agree that they are both dealing with the ontological fundamental of relationality—the irrevocable connectedness between the members of a relationship, as described above. Both theology and psychology deal fundamentally with relationships. Theology describes the relationship between God and us. Describing the nature of God independent of God's relationship to us is totally irrelevant, intellectually meaningless, and at best a form of intellectual masturbation. Psychology is the science that describes how our personalities developed from our experience in relationships and develops psychotherapies to change the destructive aspects of that experience. Psychology also describes the relationship between our minds, our bodies, and the outside world. Acknowledging the ontological fundamental of relationality allows both psychology and theology to use a common intellectual foundation for the scientific work on natural phenomena. Ontological relationality appears to describe reality best at this time in history. It also facilitates the inclusion of spirituality based on relationships; i.e., the loving and destructive ways we treat ourselves, others, the earth, and our relationship with God.

Using this common worldview will facilitate healing and release from the slavery of sin by Christians and others because it emphasizes compassion. It can also stop unnecessary debate between psychology, theology, and Church practice.

I do not claim that my theory of idolatrous images is the only viable psychological concept to describe the etiology of sin. My understanding of the etiology of sin is one way that psychology can inform theology, preaching, the sacrament of penance, and Church teaching. However, using my etiology of sin, most theologians and Church teachings do not acknowledge the experience in relationships. Yet it is common knowledge that we often act like our parents; psychological research verifies how children often act like their parents or abusers. It seems imperative that theologians, clergy, and Church teachings use modern psychological concepts in order to help the faithful get relief from the slavery to sin, as psychologists do. I have heard many preachers tell the congregation that they were sinners. They were condemning without any sense of compassion for the difficulty of slavery to sin, and made no suggestions of how to become more loving except to say, "You need to stop sinning." Hence, it is important to change the traditional definition of sin, because it can help free us from the slavery to our attachments, our behavior, and our guilt and shame. We are not responsible for our disposition to sin, but we need to take responsibility for the sin we commit. It is time for those theologians, clergy, and pastoral ministers who judge people as sinners to be more compassionate with those who are trying to free themselves from slavery to sin.

Confession is a common activity in both psychotherapy and Christian practice. Some churches encourage sacramental confession of sins. All psychotherapists also hear confessions of sin regularly. Confession is essential for healing because it exposes a secret to another person. In this sense, it is appropriate to say that the confessor is an intermediary between us and God. God is the one who forgives sin, but the confessor or the psychotherapist is the earthly agent. They listen to our confession of shame and guilt in order for us to hear that we are relieved of the burden of our sin. Then we know that we are not alone and that we need others and God to be free of sin. Yet confession is only a start, because compulsive sin will be repeated until the attachment to the idolatrous image is severed. Hence, church teaching about sacramental confession ought to include a means to detach from the idolatrous images that produce sin, not just the confession of sin.

Psychological insights about shame and guilt also have significant implications for theology, preaching, sacramental confession, and Christian ministry. We feel guilty when we believe that we did something wrong. Shame is a *belief* that we are bad because we did something wrong. Guilt is about an act; shame is about who we become as a result. Guilt is helpful because it gets our attention, like hitting a jackass with a two-by-four. When we feel guilt, we automatically feel shame because we have no defense that differentiates what we do from who we are. Some people feel guilt and shame because they are perfectionistic (or scrupulous) or have a guilty conscience. After we feel the guilt, we need to let ourselves be forgiven and learn how to stop the sin. Holding onto it only tortures us and feeds our shame. Unless it can be determined that people actually did something wrong to warrant the intensity of the guilt, this is pseudoguilt. A preoccupation with shame usually results from family systems that promote toxic shame and an obsession with morality. John Bradshaw (1990) writes about toxic shame in families caused by vulnerable children being hurt, abandoned, shamed, or neglected. However, there is also healthy shame. Carol Bohn (2002) gave a presentation on shame that identified healthy and destructive shame. Shame is our affective response to others. If we feel ashamed of what we did to others by addictions, hurting someone, stealing, or other abusive acts, this shame reminds us that we hurt them. It helps us take responsibility for sinful behavior. Healthy shame counterbalances narcissism. Unhealthy shame is a belief that we are bad people because we sinned or were abused, neglected, or abandoned. This shame impedes our freedom, enslaves us to destructive beliefs, and paralyzes healthy self-esteem. In addition, it disposes us to repeat sinful behavior that acts out the belief. However, there is a stage of psychospiritual development where guilt does not always turn to shame—the stage of unconditional self-love.

The stage of unconditional self-love is achieved by letting go of our attachments to our idolatrous images. These attachments keep the relational self identified with, or enslaved to, the conditional self-love of our experience; i.e., stuck in shame. Our attachments create conditional self-love because they tell us that we can only be loved *if* we are always perfect, *if* we follow our parents' rules, *if* we always get good grades, or *if* we never act out with drugs, sex, or money, hurt someone, and the like.

We become unconditionally self-loving when we choose to stop repeating the old relationship in current relationships by discovering the fundamental belief that keeps us stuck to the idolatrous images. My experience is a good example of this change to unconditional self-love. During a supervision session at The Inter-Faith Counseling Center of Greater New Bedford, I was processing critical feedback from other therapists about a case presentation to them. I was devastated by their criticism and felt incompetent because I was criticized. As my supervisor questioned what was behind this profound sense of incompetence, a feeling that I was unworthy of God's love overwhelmed me. Never before had I experienced any sense of this unworthiness. However, it became obvious to me that I believed I needed to be a perfect therapist to gain God's love. How absurd! It appalled me that I was still a perfectionist after all those hundreds of hours of psychotherapy working on that very issue. Later I learned I was a true perfectionist when I read the January 2 quote in *Touchstones* (Hazelden, 1986): "When you can't stand criticism you learn to be a perfectionist." I was freed from my slavery to perfectionism because I learned that the belief, "I am unworthy of God's love," was the foundation for my perfectionism. Since then my perfectionism has died, and I am not preoccupied with pleasing people. Now when I do something wrong, I am not overwhelmed by guilt or shame; I do feel guilty, but that guilt does not turn to shame. Instead, I ask myself, "What can I learn from doing this, so I don't repeat it?" Feeling guilt but not shame is the criterion to differentiate conditional from unconditional self-love. Many people in twelve-step programs experience this stage of development if they relapse after the intense compulsion of the addiction has subsided. They do not experience self-hatred at this time because they have become identified with their whole relational self, not just the idolatrous image. Healthy self-esteem replaces self-hatred and negative thinking.

Following is my psychotheological statement about sin, original sin, will, shame, guilt, unconditional self-love, and self-atonement. The addiction paradigm and the disease model are the best models to describe sin and how to treat it. There is evidence that sin is passed on from parents to children through genetics and experience in relationships (nature and nurture). We were born to parents who did not completely love us. Their parents incompletely loved, as were their parents back to the beginning, wherever that was. We were born both self-centered and with some capacity to be loving. We became sinful because our responses to our experience in relationships became harmful to ourselves, others, the earth, and the social order, and separated us from the incarnate presence of God. Some of our sin is compulsive; other sins are moral choices. We were not completely loved so we became incompletely loving in return. We feel guilty when we do something wrong, which turns to shame almost immediately unless we have achieved a sense of unconditional self-love. Guilt is God's way of getting our attention. Healthy shame helps us remember what we have done wrong in order to stop us from repeating compulsive sin, whereas destructive shame feeds the compulsion. Unconditional self-love is a stage of psychospiritual development where we are freed from the slavery to sin and destructive shame. This freedom enables us to learn how to stop repeating our sin. However, some self-destructive behavior like low self-esteem results in less serious consequences to self or others, but it is still sinful because it is harmful and demeaning. Low self-esteem is as much a form of pride as inordinate self-love. They both are forms of self-centeredness: low self-esteem denigrates oneself; inflated self-love denigrates others. They both separate us from God. Self-centeredness is a better term than pride, the first deadly sin, because it applies to those who have low self-esteem as well as those who have an inflated sense of self.

## The Problem of God Creating a World with Sin and Idolatrous Images

I often hear clients ask: Why me? Why did God create a world where I was abused, got sick, was neglected, where my father died, or my mother hated me so, where evil exists? Why did God give me a retarded brother who took so much attention from me? Why didn't God stop that man from abusing me? Why did I have to be born to parents like *them*? Why did God allow him to hit me so much? Do I have to live like this? These questions are addressed either directly to God or to some external Power. I am sure other psychotherapists hear similar questions.

The traditional theological answer is that God created a world with free will that led to sin and evil; evil was the result of people choosing to rebel against God and pride. Yet as I have previously said, our free will is at least compromised and often paralyzed because we are disposed to sin and have attachments and addictions. So how can that be a helpful answer? Many events are totally independent of anyone's free will, such as hurricanes, earthquakes, floods, sickness, and disasters of many kinds.

Yet these catastrophes create real psychological problems for many people. They are not just topics for idle philosophical speculation.

It is hard to explain to anyone why God made us victims of natural catastrophes or the sin of others. To answer the question implies that we can plumb the mind of God. I consider that impossible, and I know of no revelation from God to answer the question, either. The answer I often give clients is that they need to search for their own answer as part of their journey with their Higher Power. I refuse to give them a direct answer for two reasons. First, if I answer their questions, I deprive them of discovering answers for themselves by confronting God with the questions. They can learn to make sense out of their own reality. In addition, when I have tried to answer the question directly, my answer did not answer their question, anyway. I discovered that a better approach was to ask what motivated them to blame God in the first place. Second, I have learned that some clients are angry with God or blame God for tragedies because they deny being angry with their parents. Their anger at God is a displacement of their anger towards their parents or others. They refuse to get angry with the ones who produced their idolatrous images because they try to protect themselves from their intense, sometimes homicidal rage. This anger turns into resentment towards God. They maintain the resentment as resistance to letting go of their attachment to their images. For example, Larry rationalized his anger towards his parents because he understood intellectually that his parents had poor parenting skills and needed to give much attention to his very sick brother. He felt neglected and unloved by them but denied he was angry with his parents or his brother. Instead, he was very angry with God for giving him a brother who needed so much attention. Other clients blame God for their abuse and maintain resentment towards their abusers as a defense. Blaming defends them from the pain of shame, anger, or guilt. I have found it most helpful to discover why clients hold onto these feelings: this attachment is a solution to a problem even though the feelings make them miserable and enslaved to sin. I have usually discovered that clients suffer from some kind of destructive shame or a profound fear of being abandoned by the source of their shame, anger, or guilt.

The question of God creating a world where evil is possible is easier to answer. God is not responsible for the evil of uncaring, neglectful, or abusive people. We all have the option of being evil or not. God did not single out any of us for punishment because our parents sinned or because others hurt us. Jesus addressed this problem with the story of the man who was born blind at birth in John 9:2–3. "'Rabbi, was it his sin or that of his parents that caused him to be born blind?' 'Neither,' answered Jesus: 'It was no sin, either of this man or of his parents. Rather, it was to let God's works show forth in him.'"[4] "God's works," in this case, were that the man received his sight. This implies that God's healing presence can be manifested through any loss or tragedy. Our destructive relationships are simply our experience with evil that exists in the world. They are the luck of the draw. Some of us experience more abusive relationships than others. Simply, our reality is what it is. God created a world where these relationships can happen, but the One did not cause our parents or others to be uncaring, neglectful, or abusive. That behavior is their fault. In that sense, God is responsible for evil victimizing us, but the One did not leave us alone to deal with it. God knows that we are victims of sinful parents and ancestors. If we work with God and seek acceptance of our reality, then relief from suffering, healing, and joy can be realized. Complaining to God that one's world should be different only blocks the relief, healing, and joy. Accepting the sinful world the way it is, not as we would like it, creates serenity, as the Serenity Prayer says.

However, God is not responsible for the sin we committed in response to being victims. God was present with us every minute and knows what we have gone through. God does not abandon us to our sin or the evil of our world, as the Deists claim. That would make God truly sadistic. For this reason, it is easy for God to forgive us. God knows what the human condition is like; the One was present with all creatures from the beginning of creation and through the life, death, and resurrection of Jesus Christ. God sent Jesus to tell us we are loved unconditionally. Jesus Christ in the Holy Spirit is now present to forgive us. God wants us to depend on God and others, not ourselves, in order to take away our slavery to sin and to guide us to become completely loving. We have an advocate with the Father: Jesus Christ, the righteous who dwells in us through the Holy Spirit.

The Bible also has an answer to the dilemma of being born into a world where tragedies and evil occur. Christ said, "If a man wishes to come after me, he must deny his very self, take up his cross, and begin to

---

4. Some Christians have not learned this lesson yet when they say gay men got AIDS because they had sex with men.

follow in my footsteps" (Matt 16:24). I believe this self is what I call the relational self—the self-image we created in response to our experience in relationships. We are expected to strive to be loving, caring people despite the evils that happen to us. Many have demonstrated that this is possible. In Hebrews, Paul describes God as a father who disciplines, though Paul is sexist by only referring to sons. "For whom the Lord loves, he disciplines; he scourges every son he receives. Endure your trials as the discipline of God, who deals with you as sons. For what son is there whom his father does not discipline?" (12:6–7). Life is not designed to be filled with only warm fuzzies. It simply is what it is. Everyone has different problems to face, some more than others. Many problems are givens and not the result of our choices; we cannot change what happened, but we can strive to make something good or useful out of it. These passages imply that we are expected to learn a lesson from our life problems whether they are mental illness, depression, anxiety, abuse, violence, anger and rage, or the myriad other problems people face. God purposefully created a world that produces problems in order to prevent us from depending on ourselves, alone. We are brought to our knees or "hit bottom," in twelve-step lingo. We have to ask God and others for help so that we become aware of how we hurt ourselves and others.

My personal answer to the question about the relationship of God, idolatrous images, and sin contains assumptions or (more accurately) fundamental beliefs. These beliefs are the opposite of a personal heresy. We were created in the image of God with the inherent ability to know right from wrong. God gave us the inherent right to unconditional self-love, self-respect, and joy in living with others. These inherent qualities are inhibited by our response to our experience in relationships. God loves us unconditionally. We cannot earn that love. God wants us to love the One unconditionally, with all our hearts, with all our souls, and with all our minds, and our neighbors as ourselves, regardless of what happens to us—the summary of the law. The One is present with us to guide us to unconditionally love self, others, the earth, and God. We are, in truth, never alone, even though it often feels that way. We separate ourselves from the One through our sinful attachments and behavior, but the One does not separate from us. We do not want to separate ourselves from God, but we do. God tries to guide us from within, and through the events of our lives and our relationships with others to seek forgiveness for our sins. God is the source of healing and forgiveness. We can either accept the One's grace or reject it. The One does not send abuse, disease, and natural disasters to punish us for our sins or the sins of others.[5] I have often heard people say that a tragedy like a car accident or cancer must have happened for a reason. They believe God was trying to teach them something. That rationale makes God a very sadistic being. Instead, I believe that we can make something good come out of sin, disease, and natural disasters through our relationships with God, ourselves, and others. In one sense, God *is* testing us by creating a world where these things happen. The question is, Will we love God and feel happy only if we have good things happen? God simply wants us to love him regardless of what happens, so the One can manifest healing powers and presence, just as Jesus said of the man born blind (John 9:1), or even if our behavior is sinful. In the final analysis, sin, disease, and natural disasters are our reality. They simply happen. We can choose to see the love and beauty of our experience as well as the evil, or we can eclipse our life-giving experience with negativity, hatred, and resentments and poison our serenity. Acceptance of the world as it is fosters forgiveness of self and others, releases us from suffering, promotes healing, and leads us to joy in being alive. Some people construct self-hatred, some construct healthy self-esteem, and others construct malignant narcissism out of their experience in relationships.[6] These are the choices each of us make at some point in our lives.

God knows where our sin comes from. The One was there with us when we constructed the attachments and beliefs. God only asks us to seek forgiveness for our sinful acts and strive to let go of our attachment to the false idols. We need to take responsibility for our part in our current behavior and stop blaming ourselves for our victimization. It is legitimate to be angry with God for making the world as it is, but the One is not to blame for our beliefs and behavior or the evil of others. We can learn to forgive God and our abusers as a way to detach from our resentments and the reality of the trauma without repressing the

---

5. This statement is not totally true. There are times when natural disasters do result from sin, but I will not address this issue here. The biblical story of Noah and the flood is a good example of a natural disaster that is theologically attributed to sin.

6. A possible research project could determine how various people respond to being victimized. Do some develop resentments and become malignant narcissists, while others develop empathy for others? What are the different motivations? Is choice a factor?

memory in our unconscious. God can bring something magnificent out of our tragedies and sin.

## My Simple Theology

I say this as a prayer a few times a week:

Christ, in your life you were the embodiment of the law and the fulfillment of the law. In your death, the cross became the cross of our redemption. When you died, your body was given to Joseph of Arimathea and Nicodemus who wrapped you in a shroud filled with spices. They put you in a tomb, believing you died like other men, but, instead, you died to be obedient to your Father. On the third day, you rose from the dead and appeared to the women, placing them in their rightful place in creation. For forty days, you taught your disciples. You then ascended to be fully united with your Father, to be present in the Holy Spirit of God to inspire the writers of the New Testament, to be an indwelling presence to all people, and to guide the faithful remnant, as Christ the teacher.

# 6

# THE INDWELLING SPIRIT CONCEPT

I will give you a new heart and place a new spirit within
you taking from your bodies your stony hearts and giving you natural hearts. I will put my spirit within you
and make you live by my statues, careful to observe my
decrees.

—Ezekiel 36: 26–27

*Written in us is the healing guiding power to lead us on our
own path towards becoming truly caring and loving. When
we detach from our internalized images and identify with
our Indwelling Spirit, we will have a spiritual awakening—
a conversion.*

## Definition

COMING FROM THE EPISCOPAL tradition of Anglicanism, I always
considered Holy Scripture an essential part of my prayer life and
study. Prayer and study of the Bible promoted my psychological health
and spiritual growth. Almost every day since 1961, I have read a portion
of the Psalms, the Old Testament, the Epistles, and the Gospels following
the daily lectionary of The Book of Common Prayer (1977). The theology of these readings permeated my thinking and the way I lived in
relationships. Consequently, my thoughts about psychotherapy and the
Indwelling Spirit reflect this experience.

This experience led me to define the *Indwelling Spirit* on the foundation of biblical theology and as an elaboration of Roberto Assagioli's
(1965) definition of the Higher Self. My mentor, Cal Turley, introduced
me to the Higher Self concept through his psychotherapy described in

his dissertation, *Theotherapy* (1971). His theory of psychotherapy was an integration of Swedenborgian philosophy and psychosynthesis. Assagioli defined the Higher Self as the inherent guide and teacher that dwells in each of us, which he included as part of the spiritual self, but avoided connecting this concept with God. He probably wanted to define it as a purely psychological concept to avoid theological issues. In contrast, I define the Indwelling Spirit using biblical, theological, and psychological concepts. It is the inherent presence of the Triune God who teaches, guides, affirms, heals, and forgives sins, and also contains our conscience. I assume that the Indwelling Spirit is the presence of God because the Psalms and theologians use these faculties to describe God. People describe the experience of their Indwelling Spirit with these faculties. Hence, the Indwelling Spirit is an experienced phenomenon that can be the subject of psychological research.

This phenomenon is not unique to my theory. Good psychotherapists tell clients that the answers to their problems are within them. They would never say they healed their clients. The difference is that I assume answers to clients' problems emanate from the relationship with their Indwelling Spirit, not the self or the Higher Self of Assagioli. The above epigraph from Ezekiel exemplifies how the Indwelling Spirit works when anyone surrenders to it instead of identifying with the idolatrous images.

Originally, I called this concept the *Indwelling Christ*, but decided to change the name for theological reasons. The *Indwelling Christ* implies that one person of the Trinity is present, whereas the *Indwelling Spirit* implies that the Triune God is the immanent presence. Hence, the faculties of each persona of God are expressed through this psychological phenomenon.

The clearest evidence of the Indwelling Spirit as a psychological phenomenon comes from statements we often say: "I should do ____ but I don't," or "I shouldn't do ____ but I do." The blanks in these paradigm statements could include procrastination, substance abuse, gambling, eating more healthy foods, spending, studying more, being more kind to people, ceasing to hate myself, or anything that does not conform to our sense of right and wrong or healthy and unhealthy. The "I should or I shouldn't," half reflects experience with our Indwelling Spirit, and the "but I don't or I did," reflects our attachment to idolatrous images. These statements acknowledge that we know what we should or shouldn't do, but do not follow that knowledge because our attachment to idolatrous images is so powerful that they compel us to do the opposite. We ignore our own conscience and wisdom to indulge our self-destructiveness. These paradigm statements are paraphrases of St. Paul's statement about sin in Rom 7:16: "I do not do what I want to do but what I hate." He was not able to follow the law *written on his heart*, so he sinned. Exploring these statements in psychotherapy provides a gold mine of information we can use with clients to make them aware of their existing experience of the Indwelling Spirit and the feelings and behavior resulting from their attachment to idolatrous images. These statements establish both that they experienced their Indwelling Spirit and that the attachment to their idolatrous images is much more powerful. Clients then can use this knowledge to free themselves from their attachments and identify with their Indwelling Spirit. Because these statements are so ubiquitous and experiential, they can easily be the object of research about the connection between the Indwelling Spirit and the idolatrous images.[1]

The two components of the Indwelling Spirit are the presence of the Triune God and our conscience. This presence of Christ in the Holy Spirit of God dwells in everyone from conception, in both Christians and non-Christians. It is not a matter of belief but of experience. This presence is always at work, whether we acknowledge it or ignore it. It works most efficiently if we believe in its presence, or at the very least, if we follow our conscience. It strives to guide and teach us how to be in loving relationships. It affirms us and never puts us down, even when it points out our character defects or our sin. It strives to help us accept forgiveness for our sins. It provides us with the potential to grow to be unconditionally loving of ourselves, others, a Higher Power, and the earth. Our conscience is an inherent part of the Indwelling Spirit. It is not learned through our experience in relationships. Ezekiel's prediction came true: The law became written on our hearts. God planted the Indwelling Spirit in us as a saving Grace to counteract original sin. This presence unconditionally loves us, even when we sin. I learned a long time ago that the Indwelling Spirit could be affirming. A number of times I found myself cursing God for my painful depression and because many of my clients suffered grossly. Any number of times I would lie in bed pounding my pillow saying, "*God* damn you! *God* damn you!" After I stopped, exhausted, all I heard was a still, small voice say, "I love you. I love you."

---

1. I provide examples of the exploration of these paradigm statements in chapter 8.

There is, however, another voice that can be confused with the wisdom of the Indwelling Spirit—the inner critic. It is generated by our experience in uncaring and incompletely loving relationships. This voice often sounds like the Indwelling Spirit, because it tells us what we do wrong. The difference is that the critical voice causes us to feel judged for being wrong. Most often, this criticism is not even a moral issue. It is usually an internalized parent voice (the superego of Freud) that says things like, "You're always wrong; you don't do anything right." "You're just plain stupid." "You shouldn't have gotten angry that way." When we feel criticized, judged, or put down, that is the inner critic at work, not the Indwelling Spirit. The Indwelling Spirit voice never puts us down or judges us for being wrong or sinful, though it can be stern.

As I already said, even though the Indwelling Spirit is inherent, we do not always listen to its wisdom. It is possible to say that we would listen if we never experienced unloving and uncaring relationships, if all people dealt with us in completely loving ways, if no horrible things ever happened to us, and if we loved others as we loved ourselves. In other words, this world produced no sin or suffering—but that is not our reality. Our attachment to idolatrous images and the resulting behavior inhibit or paralyze the Indwelling Spirit. Nevertheless, there seems to be some connection between the idolatrous images and the Indwelling Spirit. For example, an alcoholic man was about to enter a bar. His parents had been constantly critical of him as a child, which lead him to internalize their relationship as an idolatrous image that produced self-hating beliefs and behavior. His attachment to the idolatrous image and the self-hating beliefs caused him to anaesthetize these feelings with excessive drinking. His attachment to the idolatrous image was stronger than the wisdom of his Indwelling Spirit who tried to stop him.

## The Influence of Biblical Theology on the Indwelling Spirit Concept

Since the Bible is a major source for the definition of the Indwelling Spirit, it is important to describe its biblical theology foundation. The purpose of this biblical theology is to make clear the long tradition of the immanent presence of a loving compassionate God and of references to conscience in Judeo-Christian writings. Numerous references to this tradition are contained in Genesis, the Psalms, Deuteronomy, Jeremiah, and various passages in the New Testament. The presence of God with Israel starts with the Covenant made with Adam in the Garden of Eden before the fall, then later with Noah, Abraham, Moses, and God's footstool in the Holy of Holies of the Temple in Jerusalem. The New Covenant with Christ proclaimed a new relationship with God who is present to all people, not just the Jews. In this Covenant, when we accept the unconditional love of God, the law that is written on our hearts becomes manifest in our relationships with self, others, and the created order.

The Psalms and other biblical references describe God using the same faculties I have used to define the Indwelling Spirit. For hermeneutical[2] reasons, however, it is impossible to know whether the Hebrews and Early Christians experienced the presence of God as a psychological phenomenon. The biblical record does not contain descriptions of anyone's personal experience, as we know it today. The writers of the Bible were telling the history of the relationship between God and Israel. Hence, I do not claim that these biblical passages describe an experience of my concept of the Indwelling Spirit. I am simply defining it on the foundation of this tradition because my personal experience and that of my clients and others reflects these faculties of God.

These quotations from the Psalms provide a picture of a caring, compassionate, and loving God who is immediately present to those who try to follow the Covenant. These passages do not reflect the common view that the Old Testament describes a God who is a punishing, wrathful lawgiver. The historical books and the prophets do describe that image of God, because the Israelites were not following the Covenant. These quotes contain many of the faculties of the Indwelling Spirit as I have defined it:[3]

> I will bless the Lord who gives me *counsel*;[4] my heart *teaches*
> me, night after night. I have set the Lord always before me;
> because he is at my right hand I shall not fall. (16:7–8)

---

2. I discuss this hermeneutical issue in the section, "Hermeneutics of the Indwelling Spirit," below by contrasting my use of biblical theology with Frank Lake's clinical theology.

3. I only cite a few here to make my point; I list other quotes in Appendix A. These quotes are from *The Book of Common Prayer* (1977).

4. The words in *italics* indicate the characteristics of the Indwelling Spirit present in these passages.

He makes me lie down in green pastures and leads me beside still waters. He revives my soul and *guides* me along right pathways for his Name's sake. Though I walk through the valley of the shadow of death I shall fear no evil; for *you are with me*; your rod and staff, they comfort me. (23:2–4)

He *guides* the humble in doing right and *teaches* his way to the lowly. (25:8)

For your Name's sake, O Lord, *forgive my sin,* for it is great. (25:10)

Look upon my adversity and misery and *forgive me all my sin.* (25:17)

You *speak* in my heart and say, "Seek my face." Your face, Lord, will I seek. (27:11) (God's immanent presence)

I said, "I will confess my transgressions to the Lord." Then you *forgave* me the guilt of my sin. (32:6)

I will *instruct* you and *teach* you in the way. . . . I will *guide* you with my eye. (32:9)

Our soul waits for the Lord; he is *our help and our shield.* (33:20)

*The law* of their God *is in their heart.* (37:33)

I love to do your will, O my God; *your law is deep in my heart.* (40:9) (conscience)

Create in me a clean heart, O God, and renew a *right spirit* within me. Cast me not away from your *presence* and take not your holy Spirit from me. (51:11–12)

My merciful God *comes to meet me.* (59:11) (God's immanent presence)

Yet *I am always with you*; you hold me by my right hand. You will *guide* me by your *counsel*, afterwards receive me with glory. (73:23–24)

For you, O Lord, are good and *forgiving*, and great is your love toward all who call upon you. (86:5)

The Lord shall preserve you from all evil; it is he who shall keep you safe. The Lord shall watch over your going out and your coming in, from this time forth for evermore. (121:7–8) (God's immanent presence)

> Where can I go then from your Spirit? Where can I flee from
> your *presence*? (139:6)[5]

The Psalms contain numerous references to a tradition in Judaism that describes a compassionate, loving God, provided people follow the covenant with God. There are not just one or two references, but sixty passages[6] that describe God as a caring guide, a teacher, a healer, and one who forgives sin or our conscience. They show that there was an ancient biblical theological tradition in Judaism that described God as caring, compassionate, forgiving, and immanent presence. This tradition is in dramatic contrast to the priestly tradition in which the Meeting Tent in the Sinai desert and later the Holy of Holies in the Jerusalem Temple were inaccessible to anyone except Moses, Aaron, and the Levitical priests. God was only present to Israel behind the Veil of the Temple and only accessible to the High Priest once a year. This dichotomy establishes that there were two traditions in pre-Christian Judaism: one emphasized a caring immanent presence and the other a remote immanence. It is not clear to me how these traditions coexisted in Judaism, but that issue is a subject for biblical scholars, not this book. My hunch is that the remote immanence tradition reflects an early form of clericalism promoted by the priestly cast and the immanent presence tradition comes from the Pharisees of the synagogues. However, in the New Covenant with the risen and ascended Christ, God is present to everyone and forgives sins for those who participate in the Covenant. The New Covenant is the resolution of the two traditions.

The most significant references from the New Testament to the presence of God refer to our bodies as the temple of the Holy Spirit. These passages are consistent with the Psalms. Paul writes in 1 Cor 3:16–17: "Are you not aware that you are the temple of God, and that the Spirit of God dwells in you? If anyone destroys God's temple, God will destroy him. For the temple of God is holy, and you are that temple." Later, in 1 Cor 6:13, 19–20, he writes: "Do you not see that your bodies are members of Christ? . . . You must know that your body is a temple of the Holy Spirit, who is within—the Spirit you have received from God. You are not your own. You have been purchased, and at a price. So glorify God in your

---

5. This psalm is a paraphrase of Deuteronomy 30, discussed below.
6. This number includes those in Appendix A.

body." In Eph 2:21–22, he writes, "Through him the whole structure is fitted together and takes shape as a holy temple in the Lord; in him you are being built into this temple, to become a dwelling place for God in the Spirit." These passages also imply that all of Paul's references to Christians' being members of the body of Christ suggest that the Holy Spirit dwells in them (Rom 12:4–5; 1 Cor 10:16, 12:12–27; Eph 4:25, 5:30; Col 1:18, 2:17). In other words, God now dwells in our bodies, not in the Jerusalem temple. These passages make clear that Paul believes that the Holy Spirit dwells, at the very least, in Christians. It is unclear, however, whether he believes all people are born with the Holy Spirit. These passages suggested a clearer presence of God within our bodies, which is a key faculty of my Indwelling Spirit concept. Twelve-step literature also promotes this theme. Hazelden Foundation (1986, April 4) even says that God is present in every cell of our bodies.

The references to God as *healer* come from the stories of Jesus's healing people. Almost every page of the four Gospels contains a story of Jesus healing someone. Many of those healed could be described as having mental illnesses as well as physical illnesses. Most readers know these stories so there is no need to quote them. There are stories of Jesus healing the man possessed with unclean spirits, the lepers, the woman with a flow of blood, the paralytic, the man born blind, the deaf-mute, and the epileptic, to mention only a few. These stories portray Jesus essentially as a healer, unlike all other Sages of the Axial Age. As the Risen Lord in the Holy Spirit, the primary function of Christ is healing. Hence, the role of *healer* becomes a fundamental faculty of the Indwelling Spirit in psychotherapy.

I believe it was important to quote these passages in detail in order to make it clear how the biblical tradition speaks about those who strive to overcome sin. The God who is present in our Indwelling Spirit is like the one in the psalms, not the punishing wrathful God of the priestly tradition, from Moses and the history of the judges and the prophets. The theologians of the psalms were addressing the presence of God for those who were faithful in their covenantal relationship with God, and knew that they sinned, unlike those who refused to follow the law in the stories of the Book of Judges and the prophets. They spoke of God's wrath and judgment because the Israelites refused to follow the Covenant and refused to hear the prophets' message from God, violating the law by worshipping other gods and refused to follow the tenets of justice in the law in their relations with others.

The faculty of *conscience* has a number of references in various biblical passages. The oldest references appear as *the law written on your hearts* in Deuteronomy 30:11–14.

> For this command that I enjoin on you today is not too mysterious and remote for you. It is not up in the sky, that you should say, "Who will go up in the sky to get it for us and tell us of it, that we may carry it out?" ... No, it is something very near to you, *already in your mouths and in your hearts*; you have only to carry it out.

Moses refers to *the law written on your hearts* in the context of his discourse on Israel's Covenant with God. This quote appears to emphasize the law, "this command," but here Moses is describing the law in the context of Israel's Covenant with God and the rules to maintain that relationship. Again, law, or conscience, is an inner presence in some form. In Rom 10:4–9, Paul paraphrases this passage as part of his discussion of the justification of faith in order to extend the Covenant with God to the gentiles.

> Christ is the end of the law. Through him, justice comes to everyone who believes. Moses writes of the justice that comes from the law, "The one who observes the law shall live by it." But of the justice that comes from faith he says, "Do not say in your heart, 'Who shall go up into heaven?' [that is, to bring Christ down], or 'Who shall go down into the abyss?' [that is, to bring Christ up from the dead].' What is it he does say? "*The word is near you, on your lips and in your heart*" [that is, the word of faith that we preach]. For if you confess with your lips that Jesus is Lord, and believe in your heart that God raised him from the dead, you will be saved. Faith in your heart leads to justification, confession on the lips to salvation.

Again, it appears that the law is the focus, but the primary emphasis is the new relationship with God in Jesus Christ where justice comes from the relationship with God. Christ brings the law to one's heart as a part of faith and confession.

Jeremiah and Ezekiel also refer to the New Covenant where *the law is written on your hearts* in the future. These references were references to future times because Israel continued to abandon the Covenant with God and worshipped other gods and violated the justice provisions of the law. So God sent them into exile as punishment for violating the law.

The days are coming, says the Lord, when I will make a New Covenant with the house of Israel and the house of Judah. It will not be like the covenant I made with their fathers . . . for they broke my covenant and I had to show myself their master, says the Lord. But this is the covenant that I will make with the house of Israel after those days, says the Lord. I will place my law within them, and write it upon their hearts; I will be their God and they shall be my people. No longer will they have need to teach their friends and kinsmen how to know the Lord. (Jeremiah 31:31–34)

Paul quotes this Jeremiah passage almost word for word in Hebrews 8:8–10. He says the New Covenant is present now through Jesus Christ. He says Christ is the real temple, not the one made with hands in Jerusalem. Through the life, death, and resurrection of Jesus Christ, we now have direct access to God. Now God is not just present behind the Veil of the Temple to which the High Priest had access only once a year. Christ is the mediator of the New Covenant and can save us from our sins because he was willing to die for us. He is present within us and in the heavenly temple. In other words, Paul says that Christians, at least, have a covenantal conscience; i.e., they know God and follow his commands because they have accepted Christ as their savior.

Also in Jeremiah 32:38–40:

They shall be my people, and I will be their God. One heart and one way I will give them, that they may fear me always, to their own good and that of their children after them. I will make with them an eternal covenant, never to cease doing good to them; into their hearts I will put the fear of me, that they may never depart from me. I will take delight in going good to them.

A similar passage is in Ezekiel 36:26–27:

I will give you a new heart and place a new spirit within you, taking from your bodies your stony hearts and giving you natural hearts. I will put my spirit within you and make you live by my statues, careful to observe my decrees.

The quote from Moses implies that the law is within us in some form. The other passages were prophecies of the future written to encourage the Israelites who were going into exile (in Jeremiah) and for those who would return to Palestine from exile (in Ezekiel). It was the early Christians, like St. Paul, who believed that in the New Covenant these prophesies came true: *the law was written on our hearts*. They knew God and what was right and wrong. However, these passages do suggest a long tradition of the awareness of right and wrong as some sort of psychological phenomenon.

According to George Buttrick (1962), the term *conscience*, as a psychological faculty, is explicitly used in many books of the New Testament and in Greek literature, but not in the Old Testament. He says Greek literature refers to conscience as a psychological faculty in Epicurus, Democritus, Epictetus, Philodemus, and others, as do Latin writers such as Philo and Josephus. Democritus even writes of a guilty conscience. Some of these writers were contemporaries of the New Testament times and probably affected the thinking of its writers. Conscience was not a concept in the Old Testament, except in the Wisdom of Solomon, a book of the Apocrypha.[7] In Wisdom of Solomon 17:10, "conscience emerges with a moral connotation, as a witness within man, that condemns his sin" (Buttrick, 1962, p. 671). However, this concept of conscience probably came from Hellenistic sources, not Hebrew. Hebrew thought was theocentric, not introspective or psychological. For them, wisdom came from the fear of God, not knowledge of self or examination of motives of behavior (Buttrick 1962). Hence there are no references to conscience in the Old Testament, but there are thirty-one in the New Testament, among them are John 8:9, Acts 23:1, 24:16, Romans 2:15, and many other Pauline writings, as well as 1 Peter 2:19, 3:16. These references imply that conscience is a psychological phenomenon, as I define the Indwelling Spirit, but I do not contend that their experience of conscience was the same as ours, for hermeneutical reasons.

## Hermeneutics of the Indwelling Spirit

It is impossible to say that these biblical passages refer to the experience of the Indwelling Spirit, even though they appear to imply it. There is no way to know how these early theologians experienced God because biblical literature does not describe people's experience. (Although it is possible that St. Paul's description of his sin in Rom 7:16 is experiential, but that is for biblical scholars to decide.) My purpose for including this biblical

---

7. The Apocrypha consists of books that were not part of the Old Testament because they were considered secondary, questionable, or heretical by Jewish scholars around the time of the Early Church.

theology is to make clear the biblical tradition that describes God as an indwelling presence who heals, teaches, guides, forgives sin, and is the source of our conscience when we follow God's covenant. This tradition means that some theologians for centuries have described God in this way. The hermeneutical issue is that I do not claim that those who wrote the Bible had an experience of the Indwelling Spirit as I define it. Instead, I use the faculties of this tradition to define our contemporary experience of the Indwelling Spirit. More importantly, when we listen to our Indwelling Spirit, we internalize the healing, guiding, teaching, forgiving, and conscience faculties of this tradition—making a hermeneutical leap into our experience. Or as the eleventh step of twelve-step programs says, "to improve our conscious contact with God as we understand Him, praying for knowledge of His will for us and the power to carry that out."

I make this distinction to contrast my approach to the clinical theology of Frank Lake. He projected psychological categories onto the biblical record. He identified Jesus as the perfect model of mental health. He believed Jesus exhibited psychological faculties like a secure identity because he was at unity with God. In contrast, I use the biblical tradition to define our contemporary experience of the Indwelling Spirit that exhibits the faculties of God. I avoid saying that contemporary psychological concepts are present in the biblical record.

## Biblical Theology, the Indwelling Spirit, and Psychotherapy

A reflection on the biblical theology of Krister Stendahl (1976) has implications for healing and spiritual growth through the activity of the Indwelling Spirit. In his speech to the APA, mentioned above, he reflected on Rom 7:16: "I do not do what I want to do but what I hate." He concluded that Paul was *not* describing his guilty conscience, but his concept of sin. According to Stendahl, the first description of a guilty conscience came from St. Augustine in his *Confessions*,[8] where he bewailed his guilt for an early history of debauchery. At first, I thought Stendahl meant that Christian culture had changed human consciousness by establishing *the law written on their hearts* between St. Paul's time and St. Augustine's. When I reread the article, I discovered that I

8. This assertion is not true. *The Interpreter's Dictionary of the Bible* (1962) quotes Greek sources for a similar description of a guilty conscience (pp. 671–76).

was totally mistaken. Stendahl did not imply this at all. His major thesis was that in Romans, Paul described his concept of sin as a part of his theology of justification by faith. His intent was to include the Gentiles as full members of the Early Church without having to conform to the Mosaic Law. This new understanding raised the question: If St. Augustine had a guilty conscience, why didn't Paul?

Stendahl's biblical theology made it clear there was no evidence anywhere that Paul had a guilty conscience. He even said that Paul had a "robust conscience" (p. 80). Paul describes himself as "flawless" in legal adherence to the law in Philippians 3:6. Yet he approved of the stoning of Stephen (Acts 8:1). And on his way to Damascus to arrest believers, he was struck blind after he heard a voice saying, "I am Jesus whom you are persecuting" (Acts 9:5). So why didn't Paul feel guilty for persecuting the early Christians? The answer came to me one night when I was reading Evening Prayer.[9] Paul did not suffer from a guilty conscience because he believed he was justified by faith in Jesus Christ. In Rom 8:1–2, he said as much: "There is no condemnation now for those who are in Christ Jesus. The law of the spirit, the spirit of life in Christ Jesus has freed us from the law of sin and death." He admitted that he still sinned, but his faith in Jesus Christ allowed him to accept God's forgiveness. He no longer needed to feel guilty for what he did. Paul learned that the law only said what sin was. It was a tutor till Christ came. It could not assist anyone to do justice without forgiveness and the immediate presence of Christ in the Holy Spirit of God. Justification by faith meant that he did not have to feel guilty any longer for his past sins because he followed the guidance of the Holy Spirit as detailed in Acts. Paul learned about forgiveness and justification by faith because he internalized his beliefs, just as Karen Armstrong says the Sages of the Axial Age did.

This biblical theology of Paul has profound implications for psychotherapy, sacramental confession, and spiritual direction. Most therapists and pastoral ministers are aware that people suffer from holding onto guilt, believing they are unworthy of forgiveness because their toxic shame convinces them that their past sins prevent them from being forgiven. The hermeneutical leap from Paul's concept of sin to the elimination of a guilty conscience can happen when people allow themselves to experience for-

---

9. This is another example of relationship leading to knowledge, as I said in the "Introduction." In this case, it was asking a question.

giveness for their sins and be thankful for the Higher Power who guides them. A good example of this problem is Josh. He tried to forgive himself for hurting his wife by having an affair, but could not. Through imagination exercises, he realized his inability to forgive himself was due to being punished by his internalized father. His father was a womanizer and very judgmental of him as a child. In his present life, he oscillated between the father and son roles of his internalized father relationship. He would act like his womanizing father with women; then he would criticize himself as his father did for doing something immoral, leaving him feeling guilty, unlovable, and worthless. For him, God was forgiving but always expected perfect moral behavior and punished him for his sins. He confused a loving God with his image of his father, whom he still feared. His personal heresy was remaining attached to this punishing internalized idol of his father. Hence, for him to let go of the guilt, he needed to free himself from the attachment to the internalized father relationship.

In psychological terms, people let go of guilt when they experience what keeps them attached to their guilt through a relationship with some form of a Higher Power. Step two of all twelve-step programs implies this: "Came to believe that a Power greater than ourselves could restore us to sanity." Here insanity means we hang onto guilt and toxic shame from the past. A guilty conscience creates suffering and is a sign of continued attachment to idolatrous images. However, people do not have to define their concept of a Higher Power or follow religious creeds to be successful. The second step simply means that they dedicate themselves to the process of letting go of their guilt and toxic shame by experiencing the original attachment to their idolatrous images.

In Christian theological terms, Christ is the healer in the Indwelling Spirit who facilitates the forgiveness of our sins. The Indwelling Spirit promotes the desire to confess sins; that is, to change behavior, beliefs, and attachments through psychotherapy, spiritual direction, sacramental confession, or other means. We can internalize the doctrine of justification by faith in Jesus Christ when we confess our sins and follow the guidance of our Indwelling Spirit, allowing us to be free from guilt and toxic shame. We do not have to hold onto toxic shame and guilt if we truly accept Christ's forgiveness. We can accept ourselves unconditionally even if we sin. In that conversion, we *recover* the God-given goodness of our creation and our baptism. The process of accepting this forgiveness occurs through our relationship with the Indwelling Spirit, as it was with

St. Paul. Sin still works in us but we do not have to act it out compulsively or be identified with it. We live in the Spirit, not the flesh. A loving, caring, and forgiving God is the center of our lives, *not* the law. The law kills because it condemns us for our sin, but the relationship with a forgiving God is life-giving.

In non-Christian terms, people's Inner Wisdom encourages them to seek help in loving themselves and others, and promotes unconditional love. They need to reveal any hidden secrets about what they did or feel. If they let go of their identification with internalized images and identify with their Inner Wisdom, they can learn to let go of the toxic shame and guilt. They need to identify the blocks to that identification through psychotherapy or some other activity.

The dynamics of the process are not different for Christians and non-Christians, only the name of the agent of change is different. Contrary to what some Christians claim, God does not demand acceptance of the creeds about Jesus Christ. It is only important that people do what is right and caring toward themselves, others, society, and creation. Jesus said as much: "Whoever does the will of God is my brother, my sister, my mother" (Mark 3: 35). In essence, God *prostitutes* Grace to whoever will accept it, regardless of whether they assent to creeds or not. However, the Christian vocation is to witness and proclaim the truth that God is the Power in the universe who promotes relief from the slavery and burden of sin and cares for us dearly; it is not everyone's. We acknowledge that Power as Christ in the Holy Spirit of God. Others use different words: the words to describe the process are different, but the truth is the same. This attitude towards the process of healing counteracts the egocentrism of some religious people, who believe that their religion is the true religion, which Karen Armstrong (2006) berates.[10]

Another implication of biblical theology for psychotherapy is the belief that God is wrathful. Many believe the God of the Old Testament is wrathful and the God of the New Testament is loving and forgiving. The historical books, the prophets, and even Genesis do seem to imply that God *is* wrathful. God expelled Adam and Eve from the Garden of Eden. (However, as noted earlier, this expulsion was due to disobedience.) The early Hebrew image of God truly was fearsome and wrathful. The story of Moses at Mt. Sinai pictures God as ferocious and deadly. Anyone

---

10. These religions are detailed in chapter 3, assumption 7 of theistic psychology above.

who touched the mountain would die; even animals that did so should be stoned. God only spoke directly to Moses from the smoke, lightning, and fire at the top of the mountain. Moses delivered the Ten Commandments and the Law to Israel from this direct conversation with God. No one else had this kind of relationship at that time. Here God was not an immanent, caring presence to all people. This image of God was evident during the Israelites' sojourn in the desert for forty years, when they complained about the lack of water and meat. They often rebelled against Moses and Aaron. When they came to Palestine, the stories of the early judges and the later prophets describe the wrath of God when Israel refused to stop worshipping other gods, violating the first commandment. These gods encouraged temple prostitution or demanded immolation of their children. The Israelites thus committed the sin of idolatry, which led to social injustice. They did not treat each other with caring and justice as demanded by the law of the Covenant. It was because of this injustice that the period of the judges and the prophets focused on the wrath of God. The Israelites were sent into exile because they worshipped other gods and did not follow God's justice. Yet God was always present to the Israelites from Genesis to Malachi, even when they did not follow the Covenant.

In contrast, the psalms, quoted above, describe a very different image of God. These passages make it clear that some ancient Hebrew theologians described a God who cares, guides, heals, teaches, and forgives sins. The same passages also do not imply that God expects people to be perfect, or that they can be. Hence, even in the Old Covenant, God is described with the same faculties as in the New Testament; there is no wrathful God versus a loving God.

The New Testament writings speak of a New Covenant. The law was not abrogated, but forgiveness for sins and the immediate presence of God became primary. The New Covenant no longer emphasized what was moral. Instead, it emphasized that we are forgiven for being immoral, because no one could be totally faithful to the justice requirements of the law as the Jewish community of Jesus' time interpreted it. The Gospels picture the Sadducees and Pharisees as believing that God curses sinners and that righteous people were blessed. The loving, forgiving presence of God became clearer in the New Covenant because God so loved us that Jesus was willing to die for our sins. In the Old Covenant, God always loves people whether they were good or sinful. In the New Covenant, the relationship with God was emphasized over the morality of the law because it is impossible to be moral without God's help. Being moral—keeping the law—comes because we surrender to God, which is our response to the tremendous gift of love by the death and resurrection of Jesus Christ. We cannot be moral by our own unaided will, despite claims to the contrary.[11] We feel so loved that we strive not to sin, and God helps us do that. Every human being is the beneficiary of this new picture of God's love, regardless of whether they believe it or not. Many respond with thanksgiving and moral behavior, as Christians do, without knowing this truth.

Hence, it is not accurate to say that the Old Covenant is about the law delivered by a wrathful God and the New Covenant is about faith in a loving God. The historical books and the prophets describe a wrathful God because the Israelites repeatedly disobeyed the Covenant. The psalms describe a compassionate God because these theologians were *striving to live* the Covenant, even after they went into exile in Babylon. Jesus expresses the compassion of God to sinners and the afflicted. He tells them to sin no more. However, he condemns the Pharisees, Sadducees, and the privileged for being hypocrites, because they followed the letter of the law, not the commandments for justice, particularly with the poor and the sinners.

This biblical theology means that God can be merciful to some and wrathful to others. God is merciful to those who admit they sin and ask for forgiveness but wrathful to those who sin but do not ask for forgiveness. If we sin, God does not reject us. We move away from God until we ask for forgiveness. When we continue to sin and ignore the guidance of our Indwelling Spirit, we experience pain and suffering until we ask for help and forgiveness. However, this suffering is the consequence of our sin, not of God's wrath in these experiences; God is not being a wrathful-law giver. It is a common human experience. However, if people continue to believe that sinful behavior such as domestic violence, murder, stealing, adultery, and perpetrating hatred is acceptable behavior, without asking for forgiveness, God's wrath becomes their experience. These people are those serial killers, sex offenders, mob hit men, and racists who never repent. Hell is a reality for them; Jesus's parable about the rich man and the beggar Lazarus (Luke 16: 19–31) says as much. Jesus was not always

---

11. If someone can become lovingly moral by her or his unaided will, I want to meet that person. Those who are loving from childhood are the beneficiaries of loving relationships; they do not choose to be loving. In this situation, I'm from Missouri. Show me!

preaching warm fuzzies; he judged the Pharisees and the Sadducees, Judas, and those who oppressed the poor.

What does this biblical theology have to do with psychotherapy? Some readers might not consider this theology relevant to psychotherapy; but it is if we look through the prism of this Judeo-Christian tradition to illuminate our current experience. This tradition is an allegory of our personal experience, not idle theological discourse. First, a change has taken place in our culture since ancient times. We no longer worship external idols of gold, silver, or wood; we now worship idols internalized from our experience in relationships. Like the Israelites, we worship other gods. Our sin is the attachment to idolatrous images, the resulting sinful behavior, and our selfishness. We are disobedient idolaters who unconsciously prefer to remain attached to our idolatrous images and the resulting sinful behavior in spite of repeated, prophetic warnings from our Indwelling Spirit. We would rather follow our idolatrous images than our Indwelling Spirit. This sinfulness casts us into an "exile" of pain and suffering, just as the Israelites were cast into exile in Babylon. If we remain attached to idolatrous images and act out sinfully, we are miserable; i.e., depressed, despondent, anxious, angry, or self-hating. Nevertheless, God is with us even when we sin. If we instead learn how we maintain our attachment to sin and listen to our Indwelling Spirit, we can become identified with it and experience the compassionate, forgiving, unconditional love of God. However, if we feel punished for our sin, it is not God who is punishing us; we are punishing ourselves because we do not follow what we know is right according to our Indwelling Spirit. God allows this suffering with the hope that pain will turn us back to the One and help us ask others for help, just as the biblical theologians described in the history of the Israelites. God is trying to get us to listen to the healing wisdom implanted in us and in our surrounding world to relieve us from the pain and suffering of our sin. God cannot help us if we continue to live a sinful way of life, but the One does exert pressure on us in various ways as Francis Thompson described in his poem, "The Hound of Heaven."[12]

Secondly, the image of God as a fearsome wrathful lawgiver inhibits the action of the Indwelling Spirit, preventing clients from experiencing

---

12. Francis Thompson (1859–1907), "The Hound of Heaven" available at www .houndsofheaven.com/thepoem.htm. When I read this poem in the early 1960s, I knew immediately it described my experience.

the grace they need. Many people believe in a judgmental, punishing god because they either learned this image of God from religious education or they confuse their parental images with their image of God, or both. This image of God has been perpetuated by many clergy and devout Christian lay people from the misunderstanding of the Old Testament, as mentioned above. Hence, people need to fire their wrathful God and allow the caring, forgiving presence of God to emerge from within them.

Now, however, the great volume of references to the presence of God in the Bible raises one big question: Why have the Churches, and most particularly the Roman Catholic Church, not made the tradition of the indwelling presence of God clearer? My answer is clericalism. I referred to this problem in the discussion of the overemphasis on crucifixion theology. It is reminiscent of the clericalism of the Sadducees, who made ritual more important than the justice of the Mosaic Law. Some priests maintain that Christ is only present to us through the Eucharist because they administer it. They become the way to the presence of Christ just like the priests of the Jerusalem Temple. These clergy have perpetrated a terrible sin, which is no different from the clerical sins of Jesus's day. They prevent people from experiencing the daily presence of a forgiving God, and these priests need to be held accountable.

## Summary: My Clinical Theology

My clinical theology says that God's presence comes to all human beings in the Indwelling Spirit. God created this phenomenon in all human beings to help us become caring and loving toward ourselves, others, and the planet, and to create a just society. The Indwelling Spirit is the presence of Christ in the Holy Spirit of God as healer, teacher, guide, forgiver of sin, and our caring conscience. This Triune God dwells in each one of us, whether we believe it or not. Some people acknowledge that presence, believe in its powers, and are healed. Others do not but are healed if they strive to be caring and compassionate. Those who believe in the goals of being caring and loving experience the compassion of God as described in the Psalms and the New Testament. Christ in the Holy Spirit of God is present in both the psychotherapist and the client to facilitate healing and moral living. Certainly, there are blocks to the Indwelling Spirit's activity in both psychotherapists and clients, but these blocks can be overcome. Psychotherapists can overcome their blocks through supervision and their own psychospiritual growth. Clients eliminate these blocks by acknowledging what they are and releasing themselves from their attachments.

Jesus Christ suffered on the cross and now dwells in us and shares the burden of our pain. He forgives our sins if we ask. We are not alone in our pain or our sins. As the Psalmist says, "He that planted the ear, does he not hear? He that formed the eye, does he not see?" (Psalm 94:9). God feels our pain when we are abused and when we abuse others.

Compulsive sins are the result of our attachment to internalized idolatrous images. Forgiveness of sins in confession and good works will not stop us from compulsive sin because those practices do not change idolatrous beliefs and behavior. Idolatrous beliefs and behavior are more powerful than the life-giving ones implied by St. Paul in Rom 7:15–16. The Indwelling Spirit calls us to know that we do not have to be enslaved by them. We all deserve to feel safe in this world because it was made for us as well as others. We have the birthright to feel loved most of the time and not lonely, or as Reinhold Neibuhr wrote in the Serenity Prayer, "[R]easonably happy in this world." The desire to stop being self-destructive is a sign that we have listened to our Indwelling Spirit and know that we cannot live a full, productive, and caring life alone. We need to ask for help from God and others. I believe God created a world where we developed various problems in order to bring us to our knees, so that we *have to* ask for this help. With help, we can bring something good out of any tragedy, disease, or traumatic experience and be thankful to the One who created us.

# 7

## A CLINICAL THEOLOGY OF SEXUAL
## RELATIONSHIPS

*Those who have AIDS are like the man born blind in John
9:3–4: "It is not that this man or his parents sinned . . . he
was born blind so that God's power might be displayed in
curing him." Jesus does not condemn sinners.*

AT THE END OF the introduction, I raised the question, Why was it important for me to identify myself as a gay psychologist in this book's
subtitle: A Gay Psychologist's Practice of Clinical Theology? The short
answer is that my experience of healing as a Christian gay man led me to
develop this Christocentric perspective.

As a gay man, I am committed to Jesus Christ as my Lord and Savior
and a desire to live a moral Christian life. I am no more holy than anyone else is. I too was a slave to sin, and still sin. In college, I embarked
on a healing journey because I felt guilt and pain from my past experience, particularly around my sexuality. This journey led me to experience
Christ as healer through my Indwelling Spirit. It taught me that Christ
was with me when I was sexually abused and even when I sinned. Christ
came to me through many hours of psychotherapy, spiritual practices,
spiritual direction, and twelve-step programs. I often felt affirmed, taught,
guided, and forgiven by my Indwelling Spirit. My therapy with Cal Turley
taught me that my problems were not the result of being a sexually-active
gay man. The problem was making myself the victim of my internalized
homophobia, the attachments to past relationships, and negative self-
messages. I was taught to discern the difference between my inner critic
and the Indwelling Spirit. I stopped trying to earn God's love and accepted
forgiveness for my sins. As a result, I was able to accept myself uncondi-

tionally, even though I continued to sin. When I sinned, I felt guilty but did not hold onto it. Instead, I was freed to learn what led to my sin in order to stop it later. This journey led to relief from depression, anxiety, perfectionism, self-hatred, shame, and slavery to compulsive sexual relationships through my relationship with Christ in the Holy Spirit of God. My healing experience was similar to what John 2:2 said, "[Jesus Christ] is himself the remedy for the defilement of our sin." Or, as Paul said in Rom 8:10–11,

> If Christ is in you the body is dead because of sin, while the spirit lives because of justice. If the Spirit of him who raised Jesus from the dead dwells in you, then he who raised Christ from the dead will bring your mortal bodies to life also, through his Spirit dwelling in you.

As a gay psychologist, I developed a theory and practice for psychotherapy based on Christian spirituality with the Indwelling Spirit as its primary concept. Since college, I had wanted to be in ministry. My healing journey started as a search to heal myself; later, it turned into a passionate desire to find a simple psychotherapy where Christ was healer. I wanted to help others find healing sooner than I did, because my homophobia and self-hatred had postponed my healing far too long. After I became free of homophobia, I was able to break the shackles of convention and to question the Christian moral theology about sexuality. However, I did not completely reject tradition. I respected the caring and loving aspects of it, which I have experienced. I was no longer subject to social conventions. I found a way to love and to have a zest for life without rejecting the fundamentals of Christian morality.

Two points are essential in explaining how I came to reconcile my sexuality with the Christian faith. First, if my healing experience and psychotherapy perspective are Christocentric, how can the Congregation of the Doctrine of the Faith of the Roman Catholic Church consider me "objectively disordered and intrinsically evil?"[1] The truth is that I could

---

1. Ironically, that phrase was contained in the "Letter to the Bishops of the Catholic Church on the Pastoral Care of Homosexual Persons," in October 1986, now called the "Halloween letter" in some gay Christian circles. It was published by the Congregation of the Doctrine of the Faith when Cardinal Ratzinger, the current Pope Benedict XVI, was the prefect. http//dignitycanada.org/halloweenletter.html. Other churches consider same-sex behavior simply sinful.

not have developed my spiritual life, experienced this healing, and developed a Christocentric Indwelling Spirit concept if I were disordered and intrinsically evil. To say this would not make sense psychologically, spiritually, or theologically.

Secondly, I do not believe people should be judged immoral because they have a same-sex orientation. Many biblical literalists cite passages to justify this judgment. John McNeill (1976) and John Boswell (1980) have tried to counter these literalists by an exhaustive analysis of those biblical passages. They said that these passages either were not referring to same-sex behavior or did not refer to the experience of gay and lesbian people in today's world. Boswell found evidence that homosexuality was accepted in various periods in Christian circles. For example, Genesis says the men of Sodom wanted to "know" the strangers who were visiting Lot. However, gay men today do not promote gang rape of anyone. In Rom 1:28, Paul says that same-sex-oriented people reject God and promote all kinds of injustice and debauchery. It is true that many same-sex-oriented people do think that one-night stands and sex outside committed relationships are moral, yet many gay and lesbian people worship God in church and pray regularly. However, my point is that analysis of biblical references is not powerful enough to change the minds of caring, God-fearing, and biblically conservative Christians. They believe homosexuality is sinful, because same-sex relationships have been considered sinful for hundreds of years. Nevertheless, there is a biblical principle that could be persuasive if it is used to make contemporary moral judgments about loving relationships—the doctrine of love as described in 1 John.

The Bible is not the only source for making moral judgments for the Roman Catholic Church; it also uses tradition. Popes have promulgated many encyclicals about sexual relationships and the immorality of same-sex people and relationships. However, neither the Bible nor theological tradition should be the only sources for determining contemporary moral judgments. Valid information can come from social-science research into people's experience. The Bible and tradition should inform moral judgments, but cannot be exclusive determinants. God's revelation was not ossified in the Bible or in doctrines promulgated by the Roman Catholic Church in the past. It continues in the experience of the faithful who reflect on the Bible and tradition. God's revelation *continues* in the life of the Church and the lives of individuals as they become more caring and loving, as suggested by Karen Armstrong (2006). A friend[2] who was brought up in the Reform Judaism tradition said they teach, "Revelation is not sealed." The Kingdom of God is a living experience, not an archive of the past. Let's remember, if the Bible were taken literally, slaves would not be free. The Bible supports slaves remaining slaves, as St. Paul says in Philemon and other New Testament letters. Many Churches of the nineteenth century did use these passages to justify slavery. Would the biblical literalists want to tell Afro-Americans that their ancestors should have remained slaves? Paul also says that women should cover their heads in temple and be quiet, and should obey their husbands. Women had no rights under the law until the twentieth century: Would the literalists like to tell women to obey those commandments? (However, some conservative ministers do say this to women.) The Roman Catholic Church and other Churches decided that slavery is wrong and that women have rights through new revelations from God about justice and civil rights, not just revelations from the Bible and tradition.

The new revelation about moral criteria for sexual relationships comes from the characteristics of loving relationships made available through social-science research. The gender of those involved and the natural theology of the past are irrelevant, even though the Congregation of the Doctrine of the Faith still uses both of these sources to decide that gay and lesbian people are "objectively disordered and intrinsically evil." There is plenty of data to support this new revelation. In contrast, James Nelson (1978) cited many psychological and theological studies that support intimacy and commitment as aspects of moral, loving sexual relationships in same-sex and opposite-sex relationships. Douglas Spina (1979) uses biological, sociological, psychological, and theological studies to argue that lesbian relationships are moral when they exhibit love with the characteristics of fidelity, commitment, intimacy, nonviolence, and generativity. Evelyn Hooker (1957) proved that psychoanalysts could not distinguish between gay and straight healthy men. The American Psychiatric Association removed homosexuality as a disorder in 1973 using her studies (1957, 1969) and many others.

2. He is James M. Saslow, PhD, a professor of art history at Queens College and the Graduate Center, City University of New York. He specializes in gay images in the history of art.

For years, many same-sex partnerships have exhibited the characteristics of love described above. Anyone who knows victims of AIDS can testify that partners and friends of these victims have been incredibly altruistic and loving towards them; many articles document examples of love between partners in the epidemic. Dignity and all the gay and lesbian Christian organizations are filled with people who worship God and strive to be moral, unlike what Paul says in Romans 2. David Nimmons (2002) cites many social-science studies that document

- That gay men are less violent than straight men.

- That gay men were the primary caretakers of their lovers and friends who suffered from AIDS epidemic during the 1980s, and still are.

- That gay men volunteer in charitable organizations disproportionately to their numbers in the population.

- That gay men are more empathetic and altruistic than straight men.

Yet to be honest, some gay men are addicted to Internet pornography as are some straight men.

While some same-sex relationships can be as moral as opposite-sex ones, the sacrament of marriage does not automatically produce moral relationships. Gay and lesbian people do not undermine straight marriages; heterosexuals do it themselves. 50 percent of marriages end in divorce. Jesus said divorce is immoral (except for infidelity, in one Gospel) and he says nothing about same-sex relationships. Yet Roman Catholic dioceses have offices called marriage tribunals that decide which marriages can be annulled. Many married people have affairs, as do same-sex people in committed relationships. Some married relationships are sources of great evil, such as domestic violence, verbal and physical abuse of children and spouses, and child molestation. Some same-sex relationships also have similar problems. Studies show that pedophiles are overwhelmingly straight, although there is a subculture of gay men who promote man-boy love.

Even the contemporary concept of *homosexuality* is not a traditional one. Jonathan Katz (1995) documented that the words *heterosexual* and *homosexual* did not appear anywhere in English until Dr. James G.

Kiernan wrote an article about perversions in 1892.[3] A year later, these words appeared in the English translation of *Psychopathia Sexualis, with Especial Reference to Contrary Sexual Instinct: A Medico-Legal Study* by Richard von Krafft-Ebing. He and other writers of that era even considered heterosexual acts perversion if they did not lead to procreation. Katz said that procreation had been the principle to judge sexual relationships in former times, not a concept of *heterosexuality*. He documented that since the late nineteenth century heterosexuality was considered dominant and good and homosexuality was a perversion. The acceptance of these terms polarized people into heterosexuals and homosexuals and was an *invention* of this era. He also made it clear that heterosexual or homosexual identity as a personality trait was also a modern invention. These identities did not exist in the sexual history of the past: then the thought world only described same-sex or opposite-sex activity. However, people did think of relationships as loving, even into Victorian times.

These references suggest that same-sex relationships have some of the same moral characteristics as opposite-sex relationships. I claim that if more research were done:

1. Both same-sex and opposite-sex relationships would exhibit the same moral criteria for love.

2. There would be no more evidence of sin in same-sex than in opposite-sex relationships.

Such research would study how the partners treat each other to determine if these relationships are loving or abusive and evil; it would study the experience of people in relationships, not whether the couple is of opposite sexes or the same sex. One confounding aspect of this research could be the argument whether same-sex orientation and behavior are matters of choice or inherent. Because it is difficult to determine whether nature or nurture determines any behavior, it is irrelevant whether same-sex relationships are the result of choice or genetics. My hypothesis is that same-sex relationships are as caring, respectful, and loving as opposite-sex relationships and that same-sex relationships are no more abusive, controlling, or demeaning; i.e., sinful or psychologically pathological, than opposite-sex relationships. These relationships would be judged based on

3. James G. Kiernan, "Responsibility in Sexual Perversion," *Chicago Medical Recorder* 3 (May 1892).

intimacy and experience with God as present in the union of the relationship, not the gender of the partners. Psychologists and theologians could work together to conduct this psychotheological research.

Since there is already evidence that some same-sex relationships exhibit love and many gay and lesbian people worship Christ, how can the Congregation of the Doctrine of the Faith of the Roman Catholic Church say that all gay and lesbian people are "objectively disordered and intrinsically evil"? The Bible and orthodox theology say that love only comes from the Holy Spirit of God. Therefore, to say all same-sex relationships are disordered and evil implies that the Holy Spirit is evil. This implication sounds like what Jesus said to the scribes about blasphemy in Mark 3:29: "Whoever blasphemes against the Holy Spirit will never be forgiven. He carries the guilt of his sin without end." He spoke thus because they had said, "He is possessed by an unclean spirit."[4] Jesus called the scribes blasphemers because they accused him of casting out demons with the power of the Beelzebub. Today Christ in the Holy Spirit of God has cast out many demons from faithful same-sex-oriented people. Yet the Magisterium of the Roman Catholic Church teaches that same-sex-oriented people are disordered and evil, even when we have loving relationships and worship God. That teaching sounds like blasphemy to me. Hence, I believe the Roman Catholic Church and other Christian Churches who teach the same have committed the unforgivable sin. They are morally bankrupt. They are the same as the scribes and Pharisees whom Jesus called blasphemers. The Roman Catholic hierarchy is morally bankrupt because they make moral pronouncements based on tradition instead of the nature of love. They insist that the Church is a holy institution, which never sins, without admitting it is *also* a human institution and thereby capable of sin.

I believe it is reprehensible to say opposite-sex marriages are holy because God instituted the sacrament of marriage. One definition of a sacrament is "an outward and visible sign of an inward and spiritual grace" (Richardson 1969, p. 300). The opposite-genders who get married in church do not make these relationships holy; the way that these people treat each other does. The churches seem to emphasize the genders of the partners and procreation more than the presence of the grace and love of God in the relationship. How are heterosexual marriages more holy to God

---

4. Similar quotes are in Luke 12:10, and Matt 12:31.

if sexual abuse, domestic violence, divorce, infidelity, and verbal abuse of partners are present and caring, committed, intimate same-sex relationships are considered disordered and evil? To say that marriage is holy and same-sex relations are evil is more an Old Covenant assertion. The Old Covenant used circumcision as the sign of the covenant. The purpose of circumcision was to create a nation founded on a covenant of justice through the procreation of marriage. That nation eventually fostered a society that lived by the law, at least after the exile in Babylon. Therefore, procreation as a definition of marriage is more in keeping with the Old Covenant than the New Covenant. Paul says the New Covenant asks for circumcision of the heart, not the body. The condition of the heart determines what kind of relationship one has, not the gender of the partners. Even Deuteronomy 10:16 says, "Circumcise your hearts, therefore and be no longer a stiff-necked people." In the New Covenant, the quality of the relationship is what matters, not the fact that it is with a man or a woman. The New Covenant talks about loving, caring relationships. All relationships—marriage, friendships or social relationships—are considered holy or sinful according to what comes out of the heart of the people involved. No one has an entirely holy relationship because all sin. Nevertheless, if both persons in a relationship strive to be loving and admit their sins and try to reconcile their differences, they can be called *holy*. This contemporary emphasis on the sanctity of marriage is relatively recent in Christian history, because, in early Christianity, celibate relations were considered more holy than marriage. It was only after the Reformation that marriage was considered as holy as celibacy.

The words of Jesus did not mention gender when he spoke about those who follow God in the Gospels as in John 3:31–36:

> For the One whom God has sent speaks the words of God; he does not ration his gift of the Spirit. The father loves the Son and has given everything over to him. Whoever believes in the Son has life eternal. Whoever disobeys the Son will not see life, but must endure the wrath of God.

There is no mention here of the gender of those who receive the Spirit. It in fact says, "He does not ration his gift of the Spirit." I think it means that the Spirit comes to anyone who will accept it, regardless of sexual orientation. John says, "*Whoever* believes in the Son has life eternal." He does not say, just those who are heterosexual. It is the person's willingness to accept the witness of Jesus Christ and follow his way that makes one holy. There are many same-sex and opposite-sex-oriented people who are caring, loving, and altruistic.

This biblical and social-science reflection can form the foundation of a new principle for sexual relationships. The moral theology of the Roman Catholic Church, which is shared by some other Churches, states that all sexual acts should be open to conception and within a marriage relationship. That means that premarital sex, masturbation, and same-sex acts are immoral. I propose to replace this principle with:

> Loving sexual relationships are moral where intimacy, commit-
> ment, mutual respect, nonviolence, a spirit of forgiveness, and
> generativity are present.

This principle deems one-night stands, sex with prostitutes, and other casual sexual relationships immoral. Love defined in these terms is the best moral principle for sexual relationships because it is based on the theological principle that God is the source of all true love. Ironically, this principle of God abiding in same and opposite-sex relationships is a cornerstone of DignityUSA's Resolution on Same-Sex Marriage (2008).[5]

The sacredness of our sexuality requires that we make love, not just have sex. God is present when love is expressed. However, this principle is an ideal. It does not mean that people need to abstain from sex before marriage or a committed relationship, but it does mean that sex for the sake of sex is immoral. If people are involved in sexual relationships that exhibit only some of these characteristics, they need to strive towards the ideal with prayer and pastoral counsel. Hence, it is more moral to have some of these characteristics than to have sex for the sake of sex or treat sex like a handshake. Masturbation is not immoral if it is a chosen act, caring of self, and not compulsive or a diversion from a healthy relationship. Compulsive masturbation would be sinful because it is done to deal with painful feelings and separates a person from relationships. However, if we do participate in sinful sexual acts, we can be forgiven as long as we promise to stop them and try to learn what motivates us to do them.

This psychotheological reflection on sexuality is an essential aspect of my perspective because sexuality is a significant factor in the lives of

---

5. This resolution was passed unanimously by the Board of Directors of Dignity USA in 2003.

all people. Any theory of psychotherapy needs to include a theory of sexuality. My theory describes sexuality with sensual, erotic, relational, procreative, and moral aspects that are to be applied to both same and opposite-sex relationships. It has no ambivalence about the essential goodness of our sexuality, because our sexuality was conceived in the image of God, as were our rational faculties. Just because we can sin with our sexuality does not make it more sinful than our reason. If reason were more moral than sexuality, rational people would be much less sinful. There is no proof of that. Most psychotherapists know that reason does not stop passions or passionate desires any more than the will does. The moral criteria for sexual relationships are the characteristics of that relationship, not the genders: Do the partners in the relationship strive for commitment, fidelity, intimacy, mutual respect and caring, nonviolence, forgiveness, and generativity? These qualities determine whether a relationship is loving and moral. Sexual relationships need not meet all these criteria at all times to be moral. The issue is: Are the partners striving to attain this ideal, just as people strive to follow the Covenant with God, but sometimes sin? However, to have sex only for its enjoyment outside a loving relationship is immoral. Pastoral guidance is needed to help people determine whether their relationship is moral when they engage in sexual relationships that do not follow all these criteria, as suggested by Spina (1979). The core principle of my clinical theology of sexuality is to affirm that a sensual, loving sexuality is an essential part of Christian spirituality, whether people are single, celibate, or in loving relationships.

8

# THE CLINICAL THEOLOGICAL PRACTICE OF MY CHRISTIAN SPIRITUALITY AND PSYCHOTHERAPY PERSPECTIVE

*Mine is not a way to truth: it is a path to connect with the author of loving truth who transforms us into loving, caring, just people.*

### Description

MY PSYCHOSPIRITUAL PERSPECTIVE IS influenced by the symptom-based theory described above by Jordan (1986) and Ecker & Hulley (1996), which focuses on the resistance of clients to change their behavior, i.e., the meaning of their defenses. The goal of my psychotherapy is to assist clients to experience the unconscious meaning of their symptoms and the meaning of their attachment to idolatrous images. It is not a solution-based approach, because I discovered that giving clients solutions does not eliminate their symptoms.

Little of this perspective is new. The new element is the use of theological, biblical, and spiritual as well as psychological concepts to describe our experience in relationship and a theory and practice of psychotherapy. My perspective is constructionist because I claim that our self-image is constructed from our experience in relationship with ourselves, our Indwelling Spirit, and other people, including our parents and other members of our family of origin and those who physically, sexually or emotionally abused us, as well as from our genetic inheritance and from our experience with our culture. Our Indwelling Spirit has participated in the construction of our self-image since our conception. The attachments to our internalized images determine much of our current behavior. When clients experience the meaning of their attachments and their symptoms, they have the opportunity to decide whether they want to perpetuate them or not. If they decide to let them go, clients relieve themselves of bondage to the attachments and the behavior that acts them out.

## Insights Gained from Using this Perspective

Recently, I discovered that clients sometimes resisted addressing their internalized idolatrous images. When I tried to focus them on these images in imagination exercises, they believed I was requiring them to address their conflicts with parents or abusers. They were not ready to deal with these conflicts. Some had ambivalent feelings about their parents. Some could not tolerate having both positive and negative feelings about their parents. Others said they already dealt with their feelings about their parents, even though it was obvious their current behavior was determined by those relationships. So now, I tell clients that we are not dealing with any current or past relationship: "Your problem is the result of the program in your brain, which was created by your experience in past relationships. Today's problem is directly related to that program, not any relationship in your past." Often I have to remind them of this distinction because they forget that we are dealing with the neuropsychological program, not the relationships that formed it.

Even if psychotherapists do not follow my perspective, it would seem helpful for all therapists to remind clients that most problems they face currently are due to internalized images, not any existing relationships. With this awareness, clients can then focus on the presenting problem instead of the resistance. And it is possible that the conflict with parents will be resolved if the client detaches from the idolatrous images instead of focusing directly on the conflict. This happened to one client who had an attachment disorder to his abusive mother, father, and his three wives. He was finally able to tolerate the gross fear of being alone and fear of abandonment when his health problems became life-threatening. He finally became sick and tired of being sick and tired. He realized that his attachment to the abusive people was exacerbating his health problems, particularly his high blood pressure. He now allows himself to set limits with all these people instead of being the victim of them. As a result, his energy level is increased, his blood pressure is down, and he respects his legitimate anger in spite of his family's resistance. It took almost four years and the consequences of many physical ailments to get to this point.

To me, the most fascinating aspect of the attachment to idolatrous images is the discovery that the connection between past behavior and current behavior is timeless. Under certain circumstances, clients act now as they did in the relationships that produced their idolatrous images, self-image, behavior, and feelings. When their current experience is similar in some way to past ones, people act out the roles of the past relationship. This pattern implies that past experience is lodged in the unconscious and determines the present behavior and feelings as if those relationships still existed. The unconscious attachment to idolatrous images promotes this replication. I call these replications of the past *emotionally reminiscent situations*. This phenomenon is proof that the unconscious is timeless. When clients become aware of this phenomenon, they start to differentiate the present from past relationships. They can say to themselves, my parents may have criticized me, but when my boss criticizes me, he is one of my parents. One excellent example was from a client who always believed she was very self-critical in intimate relationships but not in work relationships. During an imagination exercise, I asked her, "When was the first time you experienced this kind of self-criticism?" A memory flashed into her mind about the time when her alcoholic father told her that she was always bad. From then on, she constantly questioned herself. This self-doubt was exacerbated by the relentless criticism of her mother. She became a people-pleaser and always believed she was wrong, but did not know why. She chose one partner whom she manipulated and criticized. Her next partner was a man who was critical, like her parents. She believed she had no alternative but to act like her father with one partner and like the criticized child with the other, or she would end up alone; she would rather suffer now as she did as a child because this was her experience with her parents. This imagination exercise is an example of what Ecker calls "identifying the two sufferings." If she understands her two sufferings, she has the opportunity to let go of her attachment to her parents and the fear of being alone.

When clients told stories of these *emotionally reminiscent situations,* they taught me something new about internalized images. Donald Winnicott (1960), and other theorists who described introjects, implied that these only consisted of the parent or abuser objects. However, I discovered that clients would sometimes act like the abusive parent, and at other times like the child they were in that relationship. They shifted back and forth between the parent/child or victim/abuser roles of the internalized relationship. This phenomenon means that both parts of the relationship—the self and the object—were introjected together into our neuropsychological pathways, not just the parental object. This introject keeps intact the child and parent (or abuser) aspects of the relationship. I first recognized this phenomenon with Jonathan. His mother called him names and often was mean. He felt that she rejected him, but he tried very hard to please her. One of his beliefs was that "I am unlovable." In his twenties, Jonathan developed a relationship with a woman and they had a child whom he loved very much. She would often go out and leave him with the child. He believed she was having an affair and wanted to leave her, but he could not. They would have verbal and physical fights about the affair where he yelled and called her names, just as his mother did to him. After the fights, he would feel guilty and make up with her. He made amends for his behavior by paying for all household bills and food. Even though he was angry with her, he believed he could never find anyone who would love him as she did. In our sessions, he would switch from acting enraged at her to being totally unable to separate from her, sometimes within the same sentence. He moved back and forth between acting like his mother and acting as he did as a child in response to the mother's abuse. He was literally acting out the internalized image of the relationship with his mother in front of me.

This phenomenon can explain why some people who were abused become abusers, but it does not explain why some people do not. Those who were abused themselves act out on others in the role of the internalized abuser. They abuse others to gratify narcissistic needs and conscious or unconscious revenge. However, many who were abused refuse to abuse others. There is no research evidence to conclude that some experience in relationships determines that one perpetrator will abuse others and another will not. Among people with very similar experiences, some abuse others and some do not. It appears that the difference between the two groups is a matter of choice. There are only two ways anyone can act: we can act in or act out. In the first alternative, perpetrators choose to perpetrate on others if they are resentful and conclude that the world owes them something. The malignant narcissists are so angry and resentful that they have little or no empathy for anyone else, so they do not care whom they hurt. Their guilt is minimal, if present at all. Their actions are certainly sinful or evil, but it is unclear whether some perpetrators also become evil. In contrast, those with empathy for others act in. They get depressed, resentful, and self-hating but refuse to take out their anger and resentment on others. These people usually come to therapy at some time. The malignant narcissists do not come unless the court sends them or they realize they are sex addicts because they feel guilty.

The experience of clients also revealed that destructive self-esteem images are conduits of evil. However, the images are not evil in themselves; they are the pathways that the demonic uses to hurt the person and/or others, i.e., sin. Clients made it clear that the intention of these images was to make them miserable at best, or to kill them at worst. Clients were unaware that the images controlled them and that they colluded with them. It is too banal to say that these images are simply destructive. They are conduits of evil because the constructs of these images hide an intention to harm people. These images are one of the subtle ways that evil seeps into each of us under the benign guise of our experience in relationships. I believe the demonic element in our world fosters the creation of these images with the intention to destroy people. The demonic element is the destructive force that opposes the life-giving element emanating from God. Freud called similar forces *Thanatos* and *Eros*. These images contain self-beliefs that create feelings like depression, self-hatred, despair, worthlessness, and incompetence. The images are not evil in themselves but they do harm to the person and/or others, which is my definition for sin. Choose your term, *evil* or *sin*, to describe this destructiveness. Either term has the same effect on people: pain and suffering. People feel miserable and suffer greatly day after day when they collude with beliefs such as "I'm dumb, or unlovable, or no good, or worthless." I assist clients to learn that the intention of these images is to delude and overpower them, and that clients collude with them. Clients are often unaware of their role in their own suffering. This awareness helps them stop blaming themselves so much.

## Clinical Theology Practice
## with the Indwelling Spirit

Usually, the first sign of the activity of the Indwelling Spirit in psychotherapy is present in the process of deciding to come to therapy. Most clients argue with themselves about whether to come or not. They eventually decide to come because they listened to the voice that says therapy can be helpful in some way. For this reason, one of the first questions I ask clients at the first session is: What were the positive and negative thoughts you had before you decided to come to therapy? I identify the positive thoughts as their inner wisdom in order to start the process of helping them to align with their Indwelling Spirit. I refer to this experience and other similar ones in the course of therapy because I believe that the client's Indwelling Spirit is the source of healing and change. I believe the Indwelling Spirit is active when clients:

1. Follow their inner wisdom instead of their attachments.

2. Strive to change their destructive behavior.

3. Develop their own strategies for changing behavior.

4. Apply what they learned in therapy.

These changes appear to be the result of the clients' own efforts. But if I ask them, they usually describe an inner dialogue that led to the change.

In psychotherapy sessions, the Indwelling Spirit works through the relationship between the client and the therapist. Therapists are the channel of healing because they consciously connect with their own Indwelling Spirit and assist clients to connect with theirs. Therapists facilitate this connection by being caring, accepting, and nonjudgmental, like the client's Indwelling Spirit. They guide clients to experience their Indwelling Spirit as often as possible and to identify the behaviors and unconscious attachments that block access to that Spirit. There are many blocks. The most common are attachments to idolatrous images, addictions, self-hatred, unresolved grief, guilt, and shame. These blocks make people self-centered and unable to follow the urging of the Indwelling Spirit.

I am not saying that this approach is unique to me. My description is probably quite familiar to many psychotherapists. Most of us do pretty much the same thing in similar situations. I am saying that the agency of these inspirations is our Indwelling Spirit, not simply our interventions. I believe that the Indwelling Spirit uses all parts of us—our minds, our experience, our perspective—in the healing process. But the inspirations do not come solely from intellect or training. Certainly, what we say is informed by what we have learned filtered through our reason. However, I assume these interventions are from the Wisdom of the Spirit who created the universe, lived, died, rose from the dead, lives at the right hand of the God *and* dwells with us in our bodies. All those who have the gift of healing become conduits of the Indwelling Spirit who helps them guide, affirm, challenge, teach, and heal their clients. In this sense, healing through psychotherapy is a sacrament ordained by God and ministered by psychotherapists, whether they believe in the Indwelling Spirit or not.

Therapists connect with their own Indwelling Spirit by centering themselves in their bodies and focusing on the client. Prayer before the session is a valuable way of establishing this connection. Let me give you an example of listening to my Indwelling Spirit during a session. I try to maintain my connection by listening to myself and the client. However, I often cannot figure out how to help the client, as do most therapists. At these times I say to myself, "Okay, what the hell is going on here?" Then I relieve my frustration by focusing on my breathing and my body sitting in the chair. I let my whole body relax. I listen to the client. Eventually, either I find myself saying something or a thought comes to me that helps the client. I believe the source of these thoughts is my Indwelling Spirit, because I actively listen to myself and the client without analysis. I believe that these thoughts are a form of inspiration.

An experience like this happened with Bruce. He had a habit of telling stories about his family members and avoided talking about his alcoholism. I had confronted him about this habit many times in the past, but the stories persisted. One day I asked my Indwelling Spirit, "What would be helpful here? He's still telling stories." Soon it came to me: "Ask him how these stories relate to his addiction." He replied, "No one listens to me." He burst out crying because his family never listened to him and he felt misunderstood. I already knew that the emotional truth of his addiction was that his family did not listen to him and he felt misunderstood. Now he was beginning to realize for himself that his addiction was fueled by his family's lack of understanding.

I use a similar technique to assist clients to connect with their own Indwelling Spirit. I ask clients what keeps them hooked on their abusive behavior. They often say, "I don't know," within the first second after I ask the question. Then I say to them, "Please sit back in your chair. Close your eyes. Take four deep breaths and focus on your breathing. When I ask you a question, do not say, 'I don't know.' Let this question sit in your mind for a while and let your wisdom teach you." Usually they come up with an answer. I tell clients that this answer comes from their Inner Wisdom or their Indwelling Spirit, depending on their spiritual orientation. I also say that they can use this process at home. This way they can learn how to get their own answers to problems by connecting with their Indwelling Spirit.

One client admitted that she said, "I don't know" when she did not want to deal with the issue at that time, i.e., she tried to avoid it.

A good example of this technique of connecting with the Indwelling Spirit occurred with Joan. She said she felt very anxious when she was in stores crowded with people. I went through the process described above. I asked her, "What feeling comes up when you think of being in that store besides anxiety?" She said, "Anger." "Where does the anger come from?" She said that she would be unmercifully beaten when they got home if she got angry with her mother in a store. Joan appears to have generalized her fear of being angry with her mother to all public places. Generalizing the abusive situation to all similar settings is a common response to severe abuse. As a result, panic attacks happen in these settings as a defense against the unconscious memory of forbidden feelings.

Another example demonstrates how the Indwelling Spirit helps clients involved in therapy. Jane[1] was a God-centered person. She had been clean and sober for some time but was bipolar and suffered from post-traumatic stress disorder or PTSD. After a few months in therapy, she became pregnant with a third child with her current significant other. She was ambivalent about having the child, questioning whether she could be a good mother in her late forties. One day she came in feeling more anxious and depressed than usual. She admitted she had thoughts about harming the baby. She had been thinking of this for four days and had suicidal thoughts. She did not want to have an abortion and was ambivalent about adoption for the child. She felt paralyzed with her indecision. She did not want to tell anyone. She did not want to tell her doctor because she feared he would report her to the Department of Social Services. She feared the father of the child would not understand why she felt that way. She believed she had to bear this all alone. She said to herself, "I need to do things on my own because I cannot trust anyone." I asked her how she decided to come and tell me. She said that earlier she was arguing with herself about whether to come at all or tell me. "Part of me said that I should come and tell you. Another part said that I'll deal with it by myself." She said the first voice was pressuring her and she was fighting against it. Yet she denied being made to feel guilty by that voice. "It makes me feel I'm doing the right thing by telling you but I didn't feel good saying it. But I feel good now. I don't feel guilty." Naturally, I was profoundly

---

1. Jane was mentioned above in the section, "The Anatomy of Sin," in chapter 5.

touched by her trust, particularly since she had a long history of many kinds of abuse.

Jane's experience was a typical example of how the Indwelling Spirit works. Her decision to share her feelings came from her inner dialogue. The dialogue was between the powerful old self-belief voice created by her attachment to idolatrous images and the guiding voice of her Indwelling Spirit. The self-belief voice of her past fought against the guiding voice. She was able to find a way to choose the guiding voice. But most significantly, the guiding voice did not make her feel guilty about having the desire to reject her child, which is *the* characteristic sign of the Indwelling Spirit at work. However, her inner critic appeared to be absent.

## Clinical Theology Practice Techniques

This section describes various techniques I use in psychotherapy sessions to facilitate the process.

*Radical Inquiry is a technique used to determine the purpose of the symptoms.*

If clients try to change their symptom instead of learning what keeps them attached to it, they do not deconstruct their neuropsychological program that creates the destructive behavior and feelings. The result would be a repetition of the symptom in some form or its replacement by another symptom. The meaning of the attachment to the symptom almost invariably involves a grief process with the accompanying five stages of grief: denial, depression, anger, bargaining, and acceptance. This grief involves the inability of clients to accept their past experiences or certain relationships as they were. They maintain themselves as victims of past relationships through anger and resentment. They wish that their parents or abusers were different, or they want themselves to be different. Ecker & Hulley (1996) use a radical inquiry approach to assist clients to learn how their symptom functions to their benefit. They ask the following questions to facilitate this radical inquiry:

1.  What does the symptom do for clients that is valued or needed in their world?

2.  How and in what context does the symptom express or pursue a valid, important need or priority?

3. How is the symptom an actual success for the client rather than a failure?

4. To what problem is the symptom a solution or an attempt at a solution?

5. What are the unwelcome or dreaded consequences that would result from living without the symptom? (p. 158)

The intention of these questions is to experience the emotional truth connected to the symptom that perpetuates it, and to experience the constructs of the symptom imbedded in the unconscious.

A good example of radical inquiry is Noel who came in with severe anxiety about his work performance. He became very anxious when his supervisor observed his work. He was anxious because his father always criticized him as a child. His emotional truth was that he believed he never did anything right and he needed to please his father. If he did not please him, he dreaded being punished. He deconstructed his low self-esteem construct by realizing he was doing a very good job but was still reacting to his boss as if the boss were his father. He discovered that his anxiety was a cover for his anger towards his father. He acted like the child in the father/son internalized relationship by being anxious. He also acted like his father when he was self-critical.

The first step in my psychotherapy is to identify what relationship the stuck behavior was formed in. The next step is to identify the self-beliefs that are acted out in that behavior and the current relationships or situations in which the behavior occurs. The third step is to identify the feelings that maintain the stuck behavior. The process of answering these questions involves listening to the inner wisdom that comes from the Indwelling Spirit. Therefore, in order to make progress, clients need to identify the blocks that inhibit them from listening to the Indwelling Spirit in the therapy sessions and in daily life, such as addictive behavior, self-hatred, seeking love outside ourselves, fear of changing our behavior, avoiding painful history.

*Delusions are a common experience of all clients so I assist them to realize the ones they live with.*

The second step of twelve-step programs says, "Came to believe that a power greater than ourselves could restore us to sanity." A twelve-step slogan says that insanity is doing the same thing over and over again and expecting different results. The delusions listed below are typical examples of this kind of insanity. These beliefs and feelings continue despite the fact that the clients know they are untrue. They are a kind of repetition compulsion. It is very difficult to distinguish them from delusional psychosis because both defy reality. The main difference is that people with these beliefs usually recognize that these beliefs and feelings are untrue. Yet they are living in a thought world that is very similar to that of psychotic people. I tell them there are two ways of looking at reality:

1. Reality is only for those who have no imagination.

2. Reality is what is.

I prefer imagination and fantasy to reality, but reality is what we need to face.

I have used the radical inquiry approach to discover how clients constructed their delusions. Below is a list of delusions clients live by:

1. I like my nice guy self-image because it gives me a solid foundation to do what I need to do; it gives me confidence. (This man constantly questioned his judgment, avoided confrontation at all cost, and got drunk regularly because he denied he had low self-esteem.)

2. I have to keep up my macho image or I will lose ground in their eyes. (He almost lost his job because he got into a fight at work.)

3. I will be weak if I apologize for hitting him.

4. If I please her, that will keep the peace. (They constantly argued.)

5. I can change him. (A wife said this about her husband.)

6. If I don't get angry with her, she will be happy. (A man said this about his wife, who had an affair and divorced him.)

7. I can't be angry because I don't want to hurt anyone. (He is extremely self-hating.)

8. I am trying to make this unrealistic relationship work.

9. One day he will be the person I am looking for. He will feel about me the way I feel about him. (A woman is complaining about her boyfriend, who has been ambivalent about the relationship for over four years and is emotionally absent.)

10. Because he wants sex with me, he will be able to satisfy what I did not get from my parents. (An expectation remained after years of one-night stands.)

11. If I cater to him, we will not fight. (They had verbal fights continuously.)

These are but a few of the myriad delusions all of us maintain. Just about everyone suffers from one kind of delusion or another. We would have no problems if we did not have one or more delusions. The usual underlying problem is not accepting what we cannot change, as the Serenity Prayer says.

*Imagination Exercises are the most effective technique in the radical inquiry process.*

The most effective technique to determine the connection between self-constructs and idolatrous images is imagination exercises. Merle Jordan suggested these exercises during our consultation sessions. They can help answer the questions mentioned above or identify the earliest experience of the current symptom. The Indwelling Spirit can also be accessed during the exercises to help answer questions.

These exercises involve asking clients to close their eyes and remember the times they exhibited the symptom. The process of closing the eyes and going back in time is a hypnotic technique, which leads clients to access their unconscious. If the goal is to find the first time they experienced the symptom, I ask them to remember various times it occurred. Usually I know of many times when the client has experienced the symptom, so I ask them to remember these first. Then I ask them to remember others. This exercise led a client to remember that her abusive father would hit her for being a bad girl, but did not know what she did wrong. I asked her to remember the last time she had self-doubt. Then I asked her to remember the many experiences she mentioned with her significant other and with her mother. After asking her to remember five or more memories, I asked her when was the first time she remembered being hit for being bad. Almost immediately, the memory of her father hitting her flashed into her mind. She had been living out of this experience and her mother's gross criticism and rejection of her ever since, but was unaware of it. She interacts with her significant other as she did with both her parents.

If the goal is to discover the function of the symptom, the exercise starts out the same. I ask clients to remember a number of times when they experienced that symptom. Then I ask them to imagine letting go of the symptom but to observe the feelings, thoughts, or actions that prevent them from letting go. Their response answers the question about the dreaded consequences if they do not act out the symptom. In other words, they need the symptom for some reason. One example is a man who could not stop being depressed because he would lose the last vestige of the relationship with his father, who is now dead.

## The Healing Process of Psychotherapy

My personal and professional experience has proven that Cal Turley was right. He said that the healing process throughout our life forms a spiral, not a straight line, from woundedness to healthy self-love and love of others. He used a picture of a cone with a spiral path going around it from the broad base to the top point. Clients start therapy because their suffering is too great, for one reason or another. They stay in therapy for a time and the pain stops. Later, situations trigger old problems and they deal with these problems again, most often in a deeper way. They get better each time and some issues do get resolved, but this does not happen all at once. It would be impossible for almost all people who were severely traumatized as children to deal with that trauma all at once. It would be much too overwhelming and probably lethal. Hence, therapists need to be very careful not to push clients too much. The process of healing seems to be intentionally made slow by the healing powers of the Indwelling Spirit, in order to protect us. For example, I dealt with my perfectionism and self-hatred many times in many courses of therapy before I was completely healed. As I said in the introduction, for years I was anxious and depressed most of the time. Then there were longer and longer times when I was neither depressed nor anxious. Each course of therapy lessened the depression and the periods between courses of therapy became longer until I decided that I did not have to hate myself any longer, nor did I have to be perfect to get someone to love me.

## The Spiritual Goal of My Christian Psychotherapy

Twelve-step programs encourage addicts to seek a spiritual awakening in order to maintain their recovery. Carl Jung said analysis alone cannot help anyone without a spiritual renewal.[2] I believe that all people in psychotherapy need a spiritual awakening to maintain their healing process because they come in attached to idolatrous images, which are sinful. At the time they entered therapy, they do not have the freedom to *choose* to stop their destructive problems, or they would have already done so. The spiritual awakening in psychotherapy occurs when clients decide to *dedicate* themselves to discovering a life-giving program and rejecting the self-destructive one, as people do who participate in twelve-step programs. In that sense, they choose the good and reject the evil. It has been impossible for them to choose to stop their symptom because they were too enslaved to it. With this dedication, clients learn to replace their self-destructive behaviors with life-giving ones. Clients strive to create a new, life-giving neuropsychological program. They do this by connecting with their Indwelling Spirit as a teaching guide and choosing to be in relationships with kind, caring, healthy people. They know they are powerless to change themselves by themselves. They know they need others. Clients learn to accept their powerlessness as a blessing and a relief from trying to live a life determined by the internalized past. Life becomes a blessing. They know they are not completely loving, but give up perfection as a goal. They love themselves and others as they are. If they fail in their choices, they start over with help from whatever source is needed. They learn that the world can be both life-giving and destructive, but do not become overpowered by the destructiveness. They may or may not become religious or God-centered.

This spiritual goal is difficult to achieve because it means changing the unconscious, self-destructive neuropsychological programs and consciously creating a new, life-giving neuropsychological program. Changing old programs is extremely difficult for anyone, because it means changing the biochemistry of the brain. In the past, clients tried many times to change their behavior without success, because they tried to change the symptom without changing the generator of it. Their will was not free, because their attachments to idolatrous images inhibited it. If their will had been free, they would have chosen to change their behavior without psychotherapy or spiritual direction or by reading self-help books. They resisted changing their symptoms, however, because they had repressed

---

2. This relationship between AA and Carl Jung was discussed in the section, "A Brief History of Christian Spirituality Movements," in chapter 1.

the painful experiences of the past that created them. Unconsciously, they automatically acted out of that past experience without being able to choose, because their will was inhibited or paralyzed by that past. They needed help from inner resources and other people. In therapy, clients start getting the help they need. If they are wise, clients try to get help from others also, and practice daily how to eliminate negative behavior and thoughts. In this process, the therapist is a guide to their Indwelling Spirit, who in turn helps them find their own solutions to their problems. This process of getting help and support from therapists and others together with their Indwelling Spirit produces the spiritual awakening. It is not rocket science, but it is hard to do.

# 9

# SUMMARY

Now that I have finished the book, it is time to resolve the ambivalence about the kind of fool I am, as mentioned in the opening sentence of the Introduction. The ambivalence was meant as humorous. But as most people believe, critical humor hides a truth. Unconsciously, my self-critic raised its ugly head to encourage the belief that I am a *fool* to write this book. A few months ago, it even tried to encourage me to abort the project. Fortunately, I have decided to follow my Indwelling Spirit, and believe that I am a fool for Christ's sake. I thank Merle Jordan for helping me to see how I was victimizing myself again, based on my parental, internalized idols.

I began with a brief story of my personal experience because my story and my perspective are inextricably intertwined. My journey of healing through my relationship with Jesus Christ in the Holy Spirit of God was a prelude to my perspective. Christ worked within me and through many people and circumstances to help me become a clinical theologian. I am a village. As Cal Turley said, we all stand on the shoulders of the ones who preceded us. I would not be here but for all those who helped me heal and learn how to be a psychotherapist. (By now, they are all getting a little tired of my feet on their shoulders, so I am sharing my story to relieve them.)

My experience as a gay man is an essential aspect of my perspective, because I cannot separate my healing as a gay man from my profession. I am a wounded healer because I resolved many of the conflicts created by the experience with my family and my same-sex attractions. I was relieved of depression, anxiety, self-hatred, homophobia, and unworthiness through my relationship with God and many others. However, the trauma of my experience was infinitely less than the trauma of so many of my clients. Yet I was sufficiently wounded to enable me to be empathetic with their trauma. I was able to make something good come out of my pain.

During this experience, I discovered Christ in the Holy Spirit of God as the healer and the One who bears my pain while I struggled with the problems of my experience. I discovered how the Indwelling Spirit works in everyday life and in psychotherapy. My healing led me to know that Christ was with me and with myriads of other same-sex-oriented people who worship God and love others. I knew that many same-sex couples live in committed, faithful, caring, and intimate relationships and that many opposite-sex couples do not, even those who are committed Christians. This experiential evidence told me that same-sex-oriented people should never be considered "objectively disordered and intrinsically evil." To say so is blasphemy. Where love is, God is. This means that same-sex-oriented people are no more sinful or disordered than opposite-sex people. Hence, I suggest replacing the moral principle that:

- All sexual relationships are moral only if they are open to procreation for those who have received the sacrament of marriage.

with the principle that:

- All sexual relationships are moral if love is present.

Love is defined in terms of compassion, commitment, fidelity, intimacy, nonviolence, and mutuality. I suggest a research project to compare same-sex and opposite-sex couples to determine the truth of the hypothesis that both same-sex and opposite-sex couples exhibit the same characteristics of loving relationships.

Philosophically, telling my story exposes the assumptions of my psychotherapy perspective and identifies the sources for it. I expose my prejudices that arose due to my experience and, hopefully, avoid generalizing my experience to everyone else's. I claim that personal experience is legitimate data for research in psychology because our experience has profound effects on our observations and perceptions. No one can be truly objective toward what is observed or researched; the observer always has some relationship with the observed. Hence, subjective objectivity is the most accurate philosophical principle for scientific inquiry and psychotherapy, as Cal Turley suggested.

I argue for a new philosophical foundation for psychology because a subject/object epistemology ignores that the ontological fundamental reality of human experience is relationality. My study, professional training, and personal experience taught me that we are relational beings and that we cannot be totally objective. Human experience is always relational, whether we are involved in mental activity or in the world outside us. Hence, I suggest replacing the subject/object epistemology with a relational ontology. I replace the epistemological assumption, "I think, therefore I am," with the ontological assumption, "I was conceived, therefore I am." This new philosophical foundation makes psychology a relational science because *ontology* best describes the relational reality of human experience and because psychotherapy deals with the *experience in relationship* of clients. This ontology is also used to define spirituality as an essential aspect of human personality. However, this change does not mean that psychology is any less scientific. It could not exist without empirical scientific research because research is needed to determine whether hypotheses about psychological phenomena are valid or invalid. I also argue that theology needs to use the results of scientific research in its formulations, as some theologians already do.

Human personality cannot be adequately described. Personality theory can only approximate human experience. That is why there are so many personality theories. Human personality will always be a mystery just as God is a mystery, because of the nature of relationship. Relationships are to be lived, to be participated in, not totally expressed in words or abstractions. Psychologists can acquire much knowledge about human nature, but in the end, this knowledge will only approximate relationship and being. To conceive otherwise is to reify knowledge, not to relate and to be.

Psychology is in real danger of being left out of contemporary intellectual developments if it remains an epistemological science. The new paradigm in physics and philosophy identifies relationality as the ontological fundamental of reality. There is no reason to keep epistemology as the philosophical foundation of the study of human psychology because we are *relationship,* as a result of conception, inheritance, and experience.

I also argue that psychology does not have to use the amoral assumptions of rationalism in order to conduct objective, unprejudiced research. The assumptions of rationalism are no more valid for psychology than the assumptions of theism. Rationalism assumes that the created order is valueless, godless, and is governed by natural laws and principles, not relationships. The ability to be truly objective is one assumption of rationalism. Theism, in contrast, assumes that the created order is value-laden and that God is active in the world, including the relationships of human experience. The assumptions of rationalism ignore the obvious fact that human experience is value-laden. Despite this assumption, however, psychologists use value-laden terminology, such as "destructive behavior" or "healthy/unhealthy behavior" or "criminal behavior," while claiming that psychology is valueless. They chose these terms to avoid the concepts of morality, such as "sin," because they wanted to avoid being judgmental and prejudiced. However, some behaviors like pedophilia or murder should be called bad or evil, and we can do so without distorting any reality or preventing valid research exploration of the subject. After all, Otto Kernberg (1993) calls some criminals malignant narcissists, an extremely value-laden term. Hence, it is possible to have a theistic psychology without destroying the validity of empirical research, if the assumptions of theism are made explicit.

In a theistic psychology, one assumption is that some form of a Higher Power is present in the psychotherapeutic relationship, and is the source of healing. If psychologists deny this presence, clients and therapists are robbed of conscious participation with a true power of healing. This Higher Power is a real power, not just a theory. I suggest research to explore the activity of this Power in psychotherapy. It is utter hubris for psychotherapists to believe that the therapeutic relationship and various psychological techniques are the *only* sources that facilitate healing. Healing and growth occur when clients struggle with the crisis they face and where the therapist becomes a conduit of this healing power, even if the client and the therapist are unaware of that presence.

Because psychologists have avoided dealing with values and morality, they have unwittingly encouraged the banality of evil. Divorcing morality from psychology has led to the compartmentalization of experience and the lack of a psychological definition of evil. It is as though evil did not exist, except in theology and religions. The psychological establishment refuses to call a spade a spade. Unwittingly, psychologists have colluded with the force in human experience—the *Thanatos* of Freud or the Shadow side of personality of Jung—that tries to destroy individuals and our culture. There is a need for psychologists to take their heads out of the sands of time and to identify what is evil behavior and suggest how to treat it. I define sin and evil as behavior that hurts self, others, or the created and social order. Some sin is compulsive behavior connected to idolatrous images, while other sin involves self-centered gratification, which has no connection with internalized images. There are numerous compulsive sins other than the serious addictions to drugs, alcohol, sex, food, and gambling, such as addiction to exercise, cars, anger, television, money, neatness, and shoplifting, to name a few. Sin-as-addiction is a preferred model, because within that framework sin loses its condemning quality without destroying the paradigm of addiction.

When psychology was a part of the discipline of philosophy, it used various concepts of spirituality and morality over the centuries. In the early twentieth century, psychology was separated from philosophy when psychologists wanted to make psychology a science like the physical sciences. In the process, they eliminated spiritual and moral concepts. Since then the history of psychology, even the pastoral counseling movement, avoided these concepts. However, there were a number of attempts to integrate psychology, spirituality, medicine, and theology, such as the Oxford Movement, Frank Lake's Clinical Theology movement in England, the Emmanuel Movement in Boston, the body/mind/spirit perspective of Alcoholics Anonymous, and the "mindfulness" approaches of Herbert Benson and Bernie Siegel. Now there are many professionals who have integrated spirituality and psychology into psychotherapy, and there is much research into spiritual and moral issues. Many psychologists and other therapists have begun to bring psychology back full circle to the integration of spirituality, psychology, and medicine, and a few have described a psychology of evil.

I suggested a number of research projects to test the following hypotheses:

1. The Indwelling Spirit is a phenomenon in human experience characterized by the faculties of its definition.

2. The Indwelling Spirit is active in psychotherapy and has an association with idolatrous images as described by the paradigm statements: "I should not do ____, but I do," or "I should do ____, but I don't."

3. Some theological doctrines have an effect on our moral behavior and our sense of self and others do not.

4. Some people internalize theological doctrines and some do not, as demonstrated by their behavior and feelings towards themselves and others.

5. Both same-sex and opposite-sex relationships exhibit the same moral criteria for love.

6. There is no more evidence of sin in same-sex than in opposite-sex relationships.

7. Some people who were victimized develop resentments and become malignant narcissists, while others develop empathy for others because some choose not to offend against others and some do.

It is unfortunate that both psychological and Christian institutions have relegated healing to the professions of medicine and psychology, for almost all religions are about healing. This separation creates compartmentalization within human personality and in our culture, in which healing comes from medicine and psychology and morality from religion. That means that people are left with the task of integration, which they often do not do. It would be much more effective for everyone if these institutions coordinated their efforts to foster a truly integrated person and culture. Psychologists and religious people could encourage the development of a community of healing to create psychotherapy that is more effective. Psychotherapy cannot heal or promote growth, spiritually or psychologically, without a community that supports healthy principles of healing and growth. Communities can facilitate or inhibit healing.

My perspective is a phenomenological Christian theistic psychology. Because it is phenomenological, it uses the terms *experience* and *relationship* as fundamental concepts. It is founded on a relational ontology because the fundamental or ontological reality of human experience is relationship, not knowledge. It rejects the traditional psychological assumptions of rationalism and replaces them with theistic assumptions. It defines the phenomenon of the *Indwelling Spirit* with psychological, spiritual, Christian theological, and biblical concepts. The assumption of this definition is that Christ in the Holy Spirit of God is present to each person and works through this phenomenon. It is assumed that God would be sadistic to leave us in this world with all its horrors without One's presence to guide, teach, and forgive our sins. These assumptions cannot be tested because they are assumptions. I also argue that theology should use a relational ontology as its philosophical foundation because the fundamental task of theology is to describe the relationship between God, us, and the created order.

Our *experience in relationships* becomes a part of us through a process of internalization. This internalization creates a composite image of all our relationships, which becomes embossed on our nervous system like a computer program—our neuropsychological program. Our response to this internalized composite image is our self-image. These images create both healthy and self-destructive beliefs about ourselves with corresponding behavior. This image consists of both the self and object aspects of the relationship, so we sometimes act like the object and sometimes as the self in that relationship. As children, we assign godlike characteristics to some of our early relationships, usually to our parents and to abusive relationships. Our attachment to these images is idolatrous because those relationships are not truly godlike. This attachment is usually unconscious and is the source of compulsive sin. Hence, we are guilty of the sin of idolatry, a violation of the first commandment.

The internalized image of our *experience in relationships* creates a unitary composite image. There is no psychological experience of this image separate from a spiritual one. This unitary experience can only be described as psychological or spiritual through abstractions. The psychological aspect of this image is the internalized relationships—the structure of the internalized image. It includes the internalized relationships and the genetic inheritance that influences self-image and behavior. The spiritual aspect of this image is the response to the internalized image, plus our potential and limitations. I define spirituality as our response to these internalized images and our Indwelling Spirit who guides, teaches, and forgives sin.

My psychotherapy theory uses a constructionist Christian spirituality. It is a constructionist approach because we construct our self-image from our *experience in relationships*. It uses Christian theological, biblical, and spiritual concepts because it is Christian theistic psychology. The psychotherapy uses a pro-symptom approach. It attempts to help clients experience the purpose they developed to maintain their symptoms, so that they will have the possibility to choose to relieve themselves from slavery to compulsive sin. The goal is not to create strategies to eliminate symptoms. The Indwelling Spirit is the major agent of healing in psychotherapy sessions and in people's lives. I believe that the Indwelling Spirit is a common phenomenon of human experience, which can be researched.

Psychotherapy provides the means to let go of the slavery to idolatrous images, with the possibility to become unconditionally loving of self, others, a Higher Power, and creation. We can learn to live in the here and now, free from destructive behaviors, conflicts, and internalized images of our past. We can learn to listen to our Indwelling Spirit and to build on the already present, life-giving internalized images. Healing occurs as we continue to listen to our Indwelling Spirit that emerges as we struggle with our problems. This Indwelling Spirit provides healing, guidance, wisdom, and a sense of safety amid the destructiveness of internalized belief systems and world events. Problems and pain are opportunities for growth and healing, or for danger and continued suffering. We can learn that the world is made for us as well as others—that we can be safe, productive, and not lonely with or without a partner. Psychotherapy can assist us to grow from self-centered gratification of needs to a balance of love of self and others, plus some kind of relationship with a Higher Power and the world.

This book is more of a critique of psychology than a condemnation, because psychology has succeeded in facilitating the healing of myriads of people, whether spirituality is consciously used or not. In addition, many psychologists and other therapists have created psychotherapies using various concepts of spirituality. The remaining problem for psychology is the reluctance of psychologists to define a psychology of evil as part of the spiritual aspect of personality theory. In contrast, this book is an indictment of the theology and practice of some Christian churches and clergy, particularly the Roman Catholic Church and other conservative churches, because they focus on morality more than on the forgiving nature of God, who is present to us through Christ's resurrection and ascension. They place too little emphasis on God's continued presence and willingness to help us in our struggles. Their theology has little to do with healing and guiding us to become more compassionate, loving, and faithful Christians. Yet, biblically, Christ is always described as a healer.

God certainly created a world where horrible things happen to many people and all of us participate in perpetuating horrors to others in some way. It is difficult-to-impossible to say why some people are victimized more than others. But then God does chasten us. We can definitely say, however, that God is present with each of us no matter what happens to us, nor what we do. We are the ones who keep ourselves from God's presence. We can also say that if we can ask help from God and others, we can bring something good out of the horrors we face. As Reinhold Neibuhr said in the conclusion to his Serenity Prayer, "You will make all things right if I surrender to your will; so that I may be reasonably happy in this life and supremely happy with you forever in the next."

# Appendix A

# OTHER REFERENCES TO GOD'S FACULTIES IN THE PSALMS

THE STATEMENTS BELOW ARE not exact quotes of each psalm. The *italicized* words are contained in the psalm verses and refer to the faculties of God that I use in the definition of the Indwelling Spirit.

| | |
|---|---|
| 25:3–4 | God *teaches* |
| 25:7–8, 11 | The Lord *guides and teaches* |
| 27:14–15 | The Lord *guides me* |
| 31:3 | For the sake of your name, *lead me and guide me* |
| 31:7 | God *knows* my affliction |
| 32:1 | *Forgiveness of sin* |
| 34:7 | God is *present to* who fear him |
| 39:9 | God *deliver me* from sin |
| 41:4 | *Heal* me for I sinned |
| 44:20–21 | *God knows* the secrets of the heart |
| 48:13 | God is *our guide* |
| 51:6–9 | Plea to *cleanse me of my sin* |
| 65:3 | God *blot out sin* |
| 66:17 | God *hears my prayers* |
| 71:12 | God's *presence* is close |
| 78:38 | *Forgive* their sin |
| 78:72 | *Guide* them |
| 79:9 | *Help* us and *forgive* us |
| 85:2 | God *forgives* iniquity |
| 90:12 | *Teach* us to number our days |
| 94:9–12 | God created our ears and eyes so God *knows our thoughts* |

| | |
|---|---|
| 99:8 | God *forgave* them |
| 103:3, 8 | God *forgives* because he is full of compassion and mercy |
| 103:13–16 | God *cares for us* because he made us |
| 116:8 | The *presence* of the lord |
| 118:6–8 | The Lord is at my side to *help me* |
| 119:33, 66, 108, 133 | I praise you and you *teach me* |
| 119:171 | You *teach me* |
| 119:151 | Lord you are *near at hand* |
| 121:1–8 | The Lord watches over each one of us to preserve us from evil |
| 130:3 | *Forgiveness* |
| 133 | The whole psalm is about *presence* |
| 141:3 | *Help me* to not do evil |
| 143:8–1 | Trust in the Lord who will *guide* |
| 145:15–20 | The Lord *helps those who fall* so call upon him for he is near |

# Appendix B

# WHAT KEEPS ME STUCK IN MY PROBLEM?

## Intake

1. Presenting problem also other incidents of the problem.
2. Family history/genogram.
3. Substance abuse history.
4. Medications.
5. Relationship history.

## Indwelling Spirit

1. Dialogue of what brought you here (pros and cons of coming).
2. Family religious or spiritual experience. o you follow it now?
3. Your image of God (compare to how parents relate to client).
4. How does God relate to you?
5. Your self-image (positive and negative beliefs about self).
6. Do you have any feelings of guilt, shame, loveable, unlovable?
7. What are your experiences of being loved or loving others?
8. How would you describe your spirituality?
9. What are other experiences of your inner wisdom?

## What Keeps Me Stuck in My Problem?

1. What is my problem and the behavior that you wish to change?
2. What is the emotional connection that keeps me stuck to this behavior pattern?
3. What relationship(s) was this behavior formed in?
4. How was I abused in that relationship(s)?
5. How have I acted our as a result of that relationship?
6. Who am I grieving? How am I grieving?
7. What current relationships are reminiscent of the victimizing relationship?
8. What ways to I try to compensate for being a victim?
9. What are you still seeking from your internalized parent or abuser?
10. What beliefs did I create for myself in response to the relationship(s) above?
    - Life-giving Self-Beliefs and Behavior
    - Self-Abusive Beliefs and Behavior

*Categories:*

Compensation (self-atonement)
Attractiveness
My body
Comparison to others
Root beliefs
Ability to be successful in the world
Intelligence
Loveability
Am I good or bad
Worthiness
Ability to relate to others

# REFERENCES

Assagioli, R. (1965). *Psychosynthesis*. New York: Hobbs, Dorman Co.

Armstrong, K. (2006). *The great transformation: The beginning of our religious traditions*. New York: Alfred A. Knopf.

Beattie, M. (1987). *Co-dependency no more*. Center City, MN: Hazelden.

Bettelheim, B. (1982). Reflections: Freud and the Soul. *New Yorker Magazine,* March 1, pp. 52–79.

Bertalanffy, L. von. (1968). *General systems theory: Foundations, development, applications* (Rev. ed.). New York: George Braziller.

Bieber, I., Bieber, T. B., and Gundlach, R. H. (1962) *Homosexuality: A psychoanalytic Study*. New York: Basic Books.

Black, C. (1981). *It will never happen to me!* Denver: MAC Publications.

Blum, H. P., Weinshel, E. M., and Rodman, F. R. (Editors) (1989). *The psychoanalytic core: Essays in honor of Leo Rangell, MD*. Madison, CT: International Universities Press.

Bohn, C. (2002). *Healthy and destructive shame*. Presentation at the Integration of Spirituality and Psychotherapy 2001–2002 Extern program at the Danielson Institute of Boston University.

Boisen, A. T. (1936). *The exploration of the inner world*. Chicago: Willett, Clark.

Boswell, John. (1980). *Christianity, social intolerance, and homosexuality: Gay people in western Europe from the beginning of the Christian era to the fourteenth century*. Chicago: University of Chicago Press.

Bradshaw, J. (1990). *Homecoming: Reclaiming and championing your inner child*. New York: Bantam Books.

Broughton, J. M., and Freeman-Moir, D. J. (Editors) (1982). *The cognitive-developmental psychology of James Mark Baldwin: Current theory and research in genetic epistemology*. Norwood, NJ: Ablex Publishing Corps.

Buck, K. S. (1998). Recent progress towards the identification of genes related to risk of alcoholism. *Mammalian Genome, 9,* pp. 927–28.

Burns, D. (1980). The perfectionist's script for self-defeat. *Psychology Today, 14,* (Nov), pp. 34–50.

Buttrick, G. A., et al. (Editors). (1962). *Interpreter's Dictionary of the Bible*. Conscience, pp. 671–76. New York: Abington Press.

Capra, F. (1996). *The web of life*. New York: An Anchor Book, published by Doubleday, Division of Bantam Doubleday Dell Publishing Group Inc.

Carnes, P. (1983). *Out of the shadows: Understanding sexual addiction*. Minneapolis, MN: CompCare Publications.

———. (1989). *Contrary to love: Helping the sexual addict*. Minneapolis, MN: CompCare Publications.

# References

Clebsch, W. A. and Jaekle, C. R. (1967). *Pastoral care in historical perspective*. New York, Harper & Row.

Combs, A. W. (1969). *Florida studies in the helping professions*. University of Florida Monographs: Social Sciences, No. 37, Gainesville: University of Florida Press.

Cross, F. L. (1974). *The Oxford dictionary of the Christian Church* (2nd ed.). London: Oxford University Press.

DignityUSA's Resolution on Same-Sex Marriage. (2008). *Quarterly Voice of DignityUSA*, *Vol 7*, No. 3, p. 1.

Driscoll, R. (1982). Their own worst enemies. *Psychology Today, 16*, (July), pp. 45–49.

Ecker, B., and Hulley, L. (1996). *Depth-oriented brief therapy*. San Francisco, CA: Jossey-Bass. Company.

Fancher, R. T. (1995). *Cultures of healing: Correcting the image of American mental health care*. New York: W. H. Freeman.

Fowler, J., and Keen, S. (1978). *Life maps: Conversations on the journey of faith*. Waco, TX: Word Books, Publishers.

Gutierrez, G. (1973). *A theology of liberation*. New York: Maryknoll Orbis Books.

Hazelden Foundation. (1986). *Touchstones: A book of daily meditations for men*. New York: Harper & Row.

Hindmarch, I. (2002). Beyond the monoamine hypothesis: mechanisms, molecules and methods. *European Psychiatry, July: 17*, Suppl. 3, pp. 294–99.

Holmes, J., and Lindley, R. (1989). *The values of psychotherapy*. Oxford: Oxford University Press.

Hooker, E. (1957). The adjustment of the male overt homosexual. *Journal of Projection Techniques, 21*, pp. 18–31.

———. (1969). Parental relations and male homosexuality in patient and non-patient Samples. *Journal of Consulting and Clinical Psychology, 33*, pp. 140–42.

Hunsberger, R. P. (2005). The American reception of Sigmund Freud. Unpublished manuscript. www.hunsberger.org/freud-america.htm.

Jordan, M. R. (1986). *Taking on the gods: The task of the pastoral counselor*. Nashville, TN: Abingdon Press.

Katz, J. N. (1995). *The invention of heterosexuality*. New York: Penguin Books USA Inc.

Kelly, G. A. (1963). *A theory of personality: The psychology of personal constructs*. NewYork: W. W. Norton.

Kelly, T. A., and Strupp, H. H. (1992). Inherent moral practice in group psychotherapy. *Journal of Consulting Psychology, 60*, (1), pp. 34–40.

Kernberg, O. (1993). *Severe personality disorders*. New Haven, CT: Yale University Press.

Kitwood, T. (1990). *Concern for others: A new psychology of conscience and morality*. London: Routledge.

Kolberg, L. (1972). Continuities and discontinuities in childhood and adult moral development revisited. In P. B. Baltes and K. W. Schaie (Eds.), *Life-span developmental psychology: Research and theory*. New York: Holt.

Kurtz, E. (1979). *Not-God: A history of Alcoholics Anonymous*. Minneapolis, MN: Hazelden Educational Materials.

McCormick, P. (1989). *Sin as addiction*. New York: Paulist Press.

McGoldrick, M., Pearce, J. K., and Giordano, J. (Eds.) (1982). *Ethnicity & family therapy*. In *The Guilford Family Therapy Series*, A. S. Gurman (Ed). New York: The Guilford Press.

McNeill, John J. (1976.) *The church and the homosexual*. Kansas City: Sheed Andrews and McMeel.

Menninger, K. (1973). *Whatever became of sin?* New York: Hawthorn Books.

Moore, T. (1992). *Care of the soul: A guide for cultivating depth and sacredness in everyday life*. New York: HarperCollins Publishers.

Mullan, H. (1991). Inherent moral practice in group psychotherapy. *International Journal of Group Psychotherapy, 41*, (2), pp. 185–97.

Nelson, J. B. (1978). *Embodiment*. Minneapolis, MN: Augsburg Publishing House.

Nelson, J. E. (1994). *Healing the split: Integrating spirit into our understanding of the mentally ill*. (Rev. ed.). Albany, NY: State University of New York Press.

Nelson, R. J. (Editor) (2006). *Biological Aggression*. Oxford: Oxford Press.

*The New American Bible*. (1971) New York: Thomas Nelson Publishers.

*The New English Bible*. (1971) New York: Cambridge University Press.

Nicholas, M. W. (1993). How to deal with moral issues in group therapy without being judgmental. *International Journal of Group Psychotherapy, 43*, (2), 205–22.

Niebuhr, R. (1964). *The nature and destiny of man*. Vol. 1. New York: Charles Scribner's Sons.

Niebuhr, R. R. (1972). *Experimental religion*. New York: Harper & Row.

Nimmons, David. (2002). *The soul beneath the skin: The unseen hearts and habits of gay men*. New York: St. Martin Press.

Norwood, R. (1985). *Women who love too much*. New York: Jeremy Tarcher.

Oliver, H. H. (1977). Theses on the relational self and the genesis of the western ego. *Theologische Zeitschrift, 33*, pp. 326–35

———. (1981). *A relational metaphysic*. Boston: Martinus Nijhoff Publishers.

Patterson, C. H. (1989). *The therapeutic relationship: Foundations for an eclectic psychology*. Monterey, CA: Brooks/Cole Publishing Co.

Peck, M. S. (1978). *The road less traveled: A new psychology of love, traditional values and spiritual growth*. New York: Simon and Schuster.

———. (1983). *People of the lie: The hope for healing human evil*. New York: Simon and Schuster.

Piaget, J. (1967). *Six psychological studies*. (Editions: Gonthier S. A., Geneva, Trans.). New York: Random House. (Original work published 1964).

Pruyser, P. (1976). *The minister as diagnostician*. Philadelphia: The Westminster Press.

Richardson, A. (Editor) (1969). *A dictionary of Christian theology*. Philadelphia: The Westminster Press.

Roberts, A. and Donaldson, J. (1926). *Ante-Nicene Christian Library*. American Reprint of the Edinburgh Edition, 1885. Charles Scribner's Sons.

Rosen, I. M. (1991). The spiritual dimension of cognitive therapy. *Journal of Religion and Health, 30*, (2), pp. 93–98.

———. (1993a). Experiences at the interface between psychiatry and religion. *Rhode Island Medicine, 76*, (2) pp. 75–77.

———. (1993b). Spiritual issues in anxiety states. *Journal of Religion and Health, 32*, (1), pp. 21–25.

Sanford, J. A. (1981). *Evil: The shadow side of reality*. New York: Crossroad Publishing Company.

Saucer, P. R. (1991). Evangelical renewal therapy: A proposal for integration of religious values into psychotherapy. *Psychological Reports, 69* (3, Pt. 2), Special Issue, pp. 1099–1106.

# References

Slife, B. D. (2005). Taking practice seriously: Toward a relational ontology. *Journal of Theoretical and Philosophical Psychology, 24*, (2), pp. 157–78.

———. (2006a). *Dare we develop a theistic science? The myth of neutrality in psychology's methods.* Paper presented at the 4th Annual Mid-Year Research Conference on Religion and Spirituality, Loyola College, Columbia, MD.

———. (2006b). *Psychology's hidden paradigm and prejudice: Naturalism.* Paper presented at the American University in Cairo, Egypt.

Stendahl, K. (1976). *Paul among Jews and gentiles.* Philadelphia: Fortress Press.

Teilhard de Chardin, P. (1959). *The phenomenon of man.* London: Wm. Collins Sons & Co. Ltd., and New York: Harper & Row, Publishers, Inc.

*The book of common prayer* (A revision of *The book of common prayer* [1928]). (1977). Kingsport, TN: Manufactured by the Kingsport Press, for New York: The Church Hymnal Corporation.

Thornton, M. (1972). *Prayer: A new encounter.* London: Hodder & Stoughton.

Turley, C. E. (1971). *Theology for theotherapy: A Swedenborgian perspective.* Unpublished doctor of ministry dissertation, School of Theology, Claremont, CA.

Van den Berg, J. H. (1970). The subject and his landscape. In H. Bloom (Ed.), *Romanticism and consciousness.* (pp. 57–65) New York: W.W. Norton and Company.

Whitehead, J. D., and Whitehead, E. E. (1994). *Shadows of the heart: A spirituality of the negative emotions.* New York: The Crossroad Publishing Co.

Whitfield, C. L. (1991). *Co-dependence: Healing the human condition.* Deerfield Beach, FL: Health Communications Inc.

Wicks, R. J., and Parsons, R. D. (Vol. Eds.) (1993). *Handbook of pastoral counseling: Vol. 2. Studies in pastoral psychology, theology, and spirituality.* New York: Paulist Press.

Williamson, W. P. (Editor). (2003). Psychology of Religion Newsletter. *Division 36 of the American Psychological Association, Vol. 28,* No.2.

———. (Editor). (2005). Psychology of Religion Newsletter. *Division 36 of the American Psychological Association, Vol. 30,* No.3.

Wood, G. (1987). *The myth of neurosis: Overcoming the illness excuse.* New York: Perennial Library/Harper & Row Publishers.

Worthington, E., Jr. (Editor) (1993). *Psychotherapy and religious values: Psychology and Christianity.* (Vol. 7). Grand Rapids, MI: Baker Book House.

Woititz, J .G. (1983). *Adult children of alcoholics.* Pompano Beach, FL: Health Communications.

Winnicott, D. W. (1960). The theory of parent-child relationship. *International Journal of Psychoanalysis, 41,* pp. 585–95.

York, R. H. (1975). *A theology towards awareness: The evil aspect of Christian platonic theology.* (Senior Thesis) Episcopal Divinity School, Cambridge, MA.

———. (1987). A new methodology to measure body/self-concept based on personal construct theory. (Doctoral dissertation, Boston University, 1987) *Dissertation Abstracts International, 48* (3), 895B.